HOW HIGH THE LARKS FLY

The harrowing but true story of a young girl
fighting to survive when her world is destroyed
by war (Latest Edition)

To Nikolai
Enjoy this book of
true courage!

HOW HIGH THE LARKS FLY

The harrowing but true story of a young girl
fighting to survive when her world is destroyed
by war (Latest Edition)

Christine Hamer-Hodges

Studio of Books LLC
5900 Balcones Drive Suite 100
Austin, Texas 78731
www.studioofbooks.org
Hotline: (254) 800-1183

Ordering Information:
Special discounts are available on quantity purchases by corporations, associations, and others. For details, contact the publisher at the address above.

Printed in the United States of America.

ISBN-13: Softcover   978-1-964148-84-7
          eBook   978-1-964148-85-4

Library of Congress Control Number: 2024911735

"Forgiveness is the fragrance the violet sheds on the heel that has crushed it" - Mark Twain

Table of Contents

ACKNOWLEDGEMENT

With grateful thanks to Penny Campbell, who introduced me to Ruth in the first place.

To Penny once again, who brought me back in touch with Barbara, Ruth's daughter, who 'had a need to know' after her Mother's passing.

Barbara has been a trove of information and an inspiration to me for finishing Ruth's story.

After Ruth died, I was in a limbo situation. I'd finished two thirds of the book. I knew the whole story, but I had a lot of "jigsaw pieces" to fit in. Barbara has been amazing, if anyone doubts anything I write about, she has -all the documents!

INTRODUCTION

I t is hard to imagine a childhood more idyllic than the one experienced by Ruth Lindenau, who lived in the Prussian village of *Tiegenort* in the early 1930's. Skating on the river in winter and sledding down snow-laden banks of the river's dam; horse-drawn sleigh rides through the village at Christmas, with all the village children wrapped up in blankets and singing Christmas Carols to the sound of tinkling sleigh-bells; rowing to her grandmother's house in summertime, down a river covered from bank to bank with flowering water-lilies and eating bread made by her best friend's father, dripping with rich butter from the local dairy, and honey collected from hives at her uncle's farm.

These are the memories which sustained Ruth when, at the age of thirteen, her entire world was turned upside down and she was chosen to become a member of Hitler's "Elite Class" and sent away from her family to live in what amounted to be a prison, to begin years of indoctrination into the fanatical workings of the Third Reich. The dubious title was given to selected children across Germany who possessed special talents and showed great academic promise; and although school district officials and the parents of the children were informed that these gifted children were being sent away for special schooling which would gain them access to the best Universities, the truth of the matter was very different.

Ruth was eleven years old when the war began. Her beloved village of *Tiegenort,* located in an area known then as West Prussia, a region inside the Polish border which had been annexed after WW1 and identified as a Free Non-Nationality State. To all intents and purposes, West Prussia was a small part of Germany surrounded by Poland. In view of this isolation from Germany, and the fact that many Polish people resided in West Prussian towns and cities, it became one of the huge bones of contention which Hitler exploited and used to set the Second World War in motion on September 1st. 1939. It all began in *Danzig,* a beautiful Prussian city known as 'The Queen of the Baltic Sea,' and the German assault on that city gave Hitler the foothold he needed to over-run and capture the entire country of Poland in his quest for *Lebensraum*, or "living space" for the expansion of Germany into Eastern Europe.

By the spring of 1945 when the war was drawing to a close, *Danzig* and the entire area surrounding it was taken by the Red Army as they advanced towards Germany, and sadly the parts of the city which had not been brought to ruins by the German Army were subsequently demolished by the Russians. By the time the war ended, seventy five percent of *Danzig* was destroyed. *Tiegenort* also became a tragic casualty of that Russian offensive, but in this case, it was the German Army who was responsible. It's location at the fork of two dammed rivers, the River *Weichsel* and the River *Tiege,* was critical to strategic maneuvers made by the fleeing occupants of the area. German soldiers broke the dam gates of both rivers and flooded the village to delay the pursuing Russian Army, giving both civilians and themselves a chance to escape. Within a few short hours, the charming little village disappeared. All that could be seen, the only thing remaining to show the world that human beings had lived there at all, was the cross at the top of the church spire. Thereafter, when the war finally ended, West Prussia became a part of Poland.

Ruth Raible told me about her life when she was 75 years old. She had vowed to her husband, Karl, that she would never discuss her past, and she kept that promise until after he died. It was an enormous burden for her, and, I believe, the experiences she kept hidden shaped her entire life. She talked about her childhood as if it was yesterday, and her memories were clear and credible. I know this, because I went to Poland and retraced her life, and everything she remembered was true. I tell this story through the eyes of a child, just as Ruth did to me. A story she kept concealed, but which had consumed her for fifty years; seared into her memory and her psyche.

This story begins, though, on a September day in 1939, when Polish citizens struggled to survive the onslaught of the Third Reich in *Danzig*, now known as *Gdansk*. The war began, as the lark flies, just forty kilometers from the beautiful little village of *Tiegenort*.

CHAPTER ONE

In the village of *Tiegenort* it was one of those mornings when everyone went outdoors to take a deep breath of fresh air. After a bitterly cold winter followed by more than a month of grey, rainy days, the sun had finally decided to come out. Although the village was still, for the most part, under a daily cloak of heavy clouds which kept it chilly in the shade, on this early spring day the light on *Landstrasse,* the only main street in the village, was welcoming and bright.

On this April day in 1940, a dazzling sky of deep azure blue dotted with scudding white clouds canopied the rural community. Blustering winds tumbled down the orderly village streets and blew over the trim rows of houses and outlying farms; twisting and tossing about loaded lines of washing, strung across lawns and gardens planted with neat rows of cabbages, potatoes and beans.

Brigitte Kruger and Ruth Lindenau, two little girls from the village aged eleven and twelve, and friends since they had been able to recognize each other as toddlers, did what they had always done on glorious Spring days such as this. They set out together early in the morning on their bicycles and pedaled quickly down the cobble-stoned village street towards the highest spot in *Tiegenort*.

The entire landscape of West Prussia, where they lived, was a flat plane, lush with rivers, marshlands and fertile soil, which made it a perfect location for farming; but the girls had a special destination in mind. They were heading for the highest "hill" in the area; an elevated grassy slope which was part of a dam that prevented the River *Weichsel* from flooding their village. Circling the pretty village church with its tall white spire, Brigitte and Ruth rode past the cemetery to a winding dirt road which led them to the foot of the grassy slope at the side of the river where they jumped off their bikes, leaving them in a tangled heap under the dam, and began to climb to the only spot in the whole vicinity where, at that time of day, they could truly feel the sun.

As they scrambled up the bank the familiar large patch of grass could clearly be seen. The sunshine had turned it into wondrous shades of yellow, indigo and emerald green; and by the time the girls were halfway towards reaching it, they could already smell the flowers. Their fragrance was almost intoxicating. Violets grew all over this part of the slope in large thick clumps; probably because after the long Northern winter the sun arrived there first and melted the snow. This was the spot the girls were heading for; as far as they were concerned it was the most beautiful place on earth.

Living in that region of Europe, so close to Russia, the inhabitants grew used to the cold climate and learned, in fact, to enjoy it. In the winter months, all the children in the village, including Brigitte and Ruth, dressed warmly in woolen hats, scarves and mittens, and dragged their colorful sleds down *Landestrasse* to this, the highest spot in the vicinity, where they spent hours sliding up and down the snow laden slope. For the children, especially the small ones, it was a huge hill, and during the endless cold weeks it provided them with entertainment from dawn to dusk. For Ruth and Brigitte though, Springtime was when they most loved being there, and they could hardly contain their enthusiasm when the sun appeared on that Spring morning to beckon them back again.

Running and scrambling up the sweet-smelling bank, Ruth and Brigitte finally reached 'their spot,' their little part of paradise where they lay down on their backs in the springing, yielding, sun-splashed grass and listened to the busy chirruping and twittering of nesting birds as they flew about collecting twigs and dry grasses for their new nests. Nature's sounds filled the air. The bucolic, peaceful mooing of cows grazing in meadows echoed all around, while the mesmerizing sound of buzzing bees and insects amongst the violets mingled with the exquisite songs of the nesting birds. For a short while at least, the two girls were transported into a world of delight; where ugly sounds did not exist, and bad things did not happen.

Shading their eyes and squinting in the sunlight, they deeply inhaled the heady perfume of violets in the warm air and gazed upwards at the great dome of heaven high above them to watch a pair of larks perform delirious soaring cartwheels in the sky.

"Look how high the larks fly." Said Brigitte, breaking their silence with a tinge of envy in her voice, "It must feel so good to be able to fly high up above the fields to another place, where nobody gets hurt and there is no fighting or killing." Ruth nodded in agreement and continued watching the birds until they flew so far into the distance, they became tiny pinprick specks in a vast space of blue.

Ruth had turned eleven six weeks after the war began, while Brigitte was one year younger. They were very close to each other, almost like sisters, for Brigitte was an only child and Ruth's sister, Gertrude, who was ten years older than she, had already left the family home, married a man named Emil Georg Steltein, and was about to give birth to her second child.

Ruth and Brigitte rolled over onto their stomachs to gaze across the sloping bank of the dam to *Tiegenort* below. It could have been a miniature dolls' village: a tiny spot of paradise flanked by two rivers which glistened pure silver in the sunlight, looking like meandering streams of mercury. At one end, the little green-painted Railway Station brought the slow-moving steam-train, the *Klein Bahn,* affectionately known by the local children as the *'choo-choo' bahn,* to the community. Near the railway station, at the top end of the village, the local dairy produced gallons of milk, butter and cheese, all of which were delivered daily by horse and cart to the village residents. The rich, creamy milk stayed cool in metal churns which clanked together as the cartwheels bumped over the cobble stones on *Landstrasse and* was measured out by the carter with a ladle and transferred into individual containers belonging to each family.

At the opposite end of the village from the Dairy, where the girls lay on the top of the dam, they had only to turn around to see their pretty white wooden Lutheran church with its tall thin spire, where they both sang in the choir and where their parents had also sung. Next to it was the dignified white painted *Pfarramt,* the home belonging to the church where visiting Ministers came to stay. Their own Minister, Pfarrer Korowski, lived in nearby *Tiegen* with his wife and two sons, Hans and Johann, two handsome young boys who were already breaking the hearts of the young village girls.

Halfway up the quaint, cobble stoned *Landstrasse* was the schoolhouse, and on either side of it, neat little houses surrounded by neat little yards filled with early blooming spring flowers. The scene painted a picture of such idyllic charm that it was impossible to believe the fact that a war filled with such hatred and rage had recently erupted just one morning's horse ride away.

Only six months prior to that day, the German Army had unleashed an artillery bombardment on *Danzig*, a town the girls knew well. They were not aware of what had exactly happened when the soldiers marched into Danzig, but they were given to understand that bad people from other countries were coming to attack *them*, and that their German soldiers would keep everyone safe.

In fact, hundreds of Polish residents in the city had been rounded up by the Germans and sent away to a Concentration Camp in *Stutthof*, a small town on the Baltic Sea where Ruth went for piano lessons, while hundreds more were taken at gunpoint to a nearby forest and executed. Although the assault on *Danzig* triggered the start of World War 11, the enormity of this action was not revealed to most Germans in the surrounding region until many months later.

Certainly, high-ranking German officials in the city of *Danzig* were well aware that the Nazis had been watching its Polish residents for some time, and were no doubt informed and prepared for the onslaught; but the average resident of West Prussia, whose job was connected with providing grains and dairy produce to the mainland of Germany, was more concerned with his or her daily life than trying to fathom the growing unrest of the people there, and the depth of Adolph Hitler's fanaticism.

Six months after that terrible day both girls were, of course, aware that their country was at war, but they were not at all sure why. Everyone they knew was given to understand that whatever was happening in the surrounding area was for the good of all the German people, and that for this they should be thankful. During the past weeks they had heard many times the sounds of explosions and the *'rat-a-tat-tat'* of armaments echoing through the valleys around *Tiegenort*; and they and their parents had not been able to go outside when night fell because of the signs posted around the village which said, *'Do Not Travel Anywhere at Night Because the Enemy Can See You.'*

They, and everyone with whom they had come into contact during their short lives, had been told to be very afraid of any soldiers other than their own German ones; who had so far been the only soldiers to enter their village. So apart from being afraid of the 'Unknown Enemy,' the girls had been somewhat shielded from the harsh realities of the situation their country was in.

Their lives revolved around attending church and school, both of which they loved; as much as they loved life in their village. The very spot they lay on was, to them, a safe place, since they had already used this sloping part of the dam as a refuge. Several times whilst cycling home in that vicinity, when they had heard the sound of air-raid warnings they had hidden for what seemed like hours, crouching beside their bicycles underneath the hill of the dam, hoping that the bombs of the enemy would not drop over their beloved village. The village which protected their homes, their families and, they trusted, their lives.

A few minutes passed before Brigitte squirmed around in the flattened imprint of grass under her body, propped her chin in her hand and looked at her friend. "What's up?" She said directly, "You've hardly said a word since we left *Landstrasse*. Is your *Papa* mad at you?" "No," snorted Ruth, "*Papa* never gets mad at me; it's *Mutti* who does that. She's always the one who tells me not to talk back, not to be out late, not to forget my homework or my piano practice and not to walk on the ice on the river; and she is the one who gets angry at me if I sometimes forget and contradict her."

"Well then," persisted Brigitte, turning back on her stomach "why are you so quiet? It's not like you. You usually don't stop talking about things. Don't you feel well?" Ruth was silent for a while, and when she finally spoke her voice had slightly changed. It was somehow quieter and lower and serious. "I feel fine. Well, sort of. In my body I'm fine, but in my mind I feel kind of angry and upset, and I don't know how to make it go away." "What happened?" Said Brigitte, getting up to face her friend, and sitting firmly cross-legged in front of her. "Well," began Ruth slowly "you know how I go on the '*choo-choo*' *bahn* to take piano lessons in *Stutthof* once a week?" "Yes," nodded Brigitte in agreement. "Well the other day when I was coming home from my lesson, we were just going past *Der Werder Hof*, my uncle Otto's big farmstead outside the village and I saw…" She paused for a moment, "You know how slowly the 'choo-choo' goes?" Brigitte nodded in agreement, and both girls smiled, recalling the large sign nailed on the inside walls of each compartment of the train; "*Passengers are Forbidden to Alight from the Train to Pick Flowers While the Train is in Motion.*"

"And I saw…" At this point in the story Ruth dropped her head and went quiet; it seemed that she would say no more. "Yes?" Brigitte prodded. "Yes? Go on. What did you see?"

"I saw something horrible." Ruth replied, and she raised her voice and frowned. "Horrible!" Brigitte's eyes and mouth opened wide in expectation. "What?" She said. "What did you see?" Ruth's answer was intense and profound. "I saw some of our soldiers in one of my uncle's fields with a line of prisoners dressed in black and white striped clothes, just like zebras, and they were pulling a cart loaded to the top with big stones. It was too heavy for even a team of horses to pull; but the prisoners were all chained together, and they were bent double trying to heave that cart along. Then, right by the side of a corn field I saw them stop, just to get breath, and the soldiers yelled at them to move on and went up to them waving their guns. Our soldiers beat the prisoners, Brigitte. They beat them with the guns until the prisoners went on pulling." Ruth's large green eyes welled up with tears. "Then a prisoner, an old man, stumbled and fell, and I wanted more than anything to get off the '*choo-choo*' and run out to go and help him; but I was very afraid because a soldier went up and struck him again and again with the butt of his gun, until somehow the old man pulled himself up and they all moved slowly away."

"Oh, Ruth," Brigitte exclaimed in horror. "That's awful!" "I know." Ruth replied, drying her eyes with a clenched fist and taking a deep breath. "It's not right." She said louder, her voice taking on an angry tone. "Nobody should treat another person like that. I didn't know that uncle Otto had prisoners working on his land; I didn't know grown-ups did that sort of thing to each other. There were so many of them, and what did the prisoners do to deserve it? One day, Brigitte, we will have to pay for treating those people in this way. It frightens me."

Otto Bremert was Ruth's Uncle, a half-brother of her mother, Augusta. He had inherited the huge farm from his father, who had died in the First World War. Augusta's mother had re-married and continued to live on the farm, where she gave birth to Augusta and another daughter, ? and the whole family took care of the land until Otto was old enough to take over.

Brigitte had never seen her friend scared before and it worried her a lot. Ruth was one year her senior and she always spoke up courageously to defend herself and her friend against anything that seemed unfair. If one of the boys in school started to bully or tease them or if they were accused by their parents or other adults of doing naughty things which they had not done, Ruth always stood up for them and was never afraid to tell the truth.

Ruth's father was the postman in their village, and Brigitte's father was the local baker, while her mother was a seamstress. By delivering the mail each day and baking the bread, their parents were heavily involved in ensuring that the ordinary, everyday things of life kept on going. Their days were busy and active with little time left over to listen to the radio or read the papers. Neither of the girls was exposed to a lot of information. They went to school, did their homework and studied hard.

When soldiers came marching through *Tiegenort* the residents made sure that the children stayed indoors. Too many young men had already been recruited to join Hitler's armies, and although no one dared say too much, lest they be reported, no parent in the village wanted to lose their child to a cause which was beginning to involve the whole of Europe.

CHAPTER TWO

By the time Ruth turned thirteen, she had grown from a child into a young beauty. Her skin was pale and clear, and her long wavy copper-colored hair perfectly complimented her large green eyes. For her age group she was much taller than average and therefore looked older than she was. She loved to ride horses on Uncle Otto's farm, and became quite a proficient rider. She liked the feeling of control she had over the horse, and how they looked together riding around the field, and then, when she had learned enough to be considered a safe rider, her Uncle had allowed her to ride along the country roads surrounding the property. Ruth already had a vision of what she wanted to do with her life. As a small child she had loved to sing and play the piano and was very gifted at both.

Her Uncle Herman, who owned a *Sattlerei* in the village where he made ropes, whips and harness equipment, was married to her father's sister, also named Augusta. As a successful businessman and lover of music he knew that Ruth possessed a talent far greater than his son, Hans, when it came to playing the piano, so in order to give Hans a little competition and encouragement, he paid for both children to have special piano lessons together in *Stutthof*, with Herr Conrad, a retired Professor of music.

Ruth loved her lessons and enjoyed the creativity of her teacher. Every few months he gathered all his students together and stood them in front of a row of wine glasses in an array of shapes and sizes. If the glasses were struck with a small metal stick, they produced amazingly melodic sounds, and Herr Conrad taught the children to play tunes on them. When the students had learned enough tunes to generate a recital, parents and relatives were invited to come and listen. Uncle Herman and Aunt Augusta would go with Ruth's parents, and they would sit enraptured, glowing with paternal pleasure and pride at the talented children they were raising. Ruth, though, had a natural talent for playing music and singing while her cousin was sluggish and lazy in his approach to education. "Watch *Ruthchen*," Uncle Herman would chide Hans as they came home together on the *klein bahn*, "she will show you how to play all the correct notes." "And practice as much as Ruthchen does, my *Hanschen*," added his mother gently, "then you will be able to play as well as her." As the only children living at home, both Hans and Ruth were quite spoiled by the adults in their lives. Hans was a sickly child who was not particularly interested in learning anything. All day long he gazed over the fields behind his house watching the farmhands at their work with the crops and the animals. All he wanted to do, was become a farmer when he left school, and he was not willing to put any effort into learning subjects in school which, he felt, did not concern him. His parents cajoled him constantly to watch his cousin Ruth and follow her example, and to that end he was placed next to her in the classroom. Ruth made it hard for him to ignore the schoolmaster by giving him a sharp nudge and a dark frown when she considered he was not paying attention.

Music was the great love of Ruth's young life, and as she got older, she was invited to play at local events or to sing solo parts with the choir at her church. Whilst doing this she discovered that she loved to perform as well. She began to pose in front of a mirror which was on a wall directly in front of her whilst she sat at the dining table. Lifting her cup very slowly with her little pinky finger bent, she watched every movement and expression she made; carefully imitating some film star or another whom she had seen at the Movie Theater in *Tiegenhof,* on one of her visits there with her grandmother. It became almost an obsession with her as she tried to perfect her actions: every sip from her cup; every forkful of food; every smile or turn of the head; each painfully slow action was observed in the mirror under her own critical gaze until her mother, Augusta, could stand it no more. Draping a cloth over the mirror she told Ruth to eat and drink properly, at the correct speed, or she would not be allowed to look in any mirror in the house for six months.

That did the trick. The mirror in front of the table remained covered, and from then on Ruth only posed and rehearsed when her mother was not watching her. She was already enjoying the sight of her budding attractiveness, and to do without it for six months was not something she wanted to tolerate. So instead of upsetting her mother with her antics, Ruth hugged her secret desire to herself. Her ambition was to entertain on stage in big cities, like Paris and Berlin; and although her country had been at war for the past two years, she clung to the hope that it would soon be over, and she could follow her dream.

It was late Spring on the day her life changed. Ruth was sitting in class when her teacher, Herr Klinger, told her that the Headmaster, Herr Kurowski, wanted to see her in his office. Ruth was a little concerned as she hurried down the corridor for her meeting, perhaps she had done something wrong or there was bad news at home, but Herr Kurowski greeted her with a smile and a word of congratulation which set her mind at rest. He explained to her that the administrative officials in *Kreis Grosses Werder*, which roughly translated means the area located all around the rivers, and was the Municipality in which *Tiegenort* was located, were offering scholarships to the top two boys and top two girls from every school in the Regional School District.

In the preceding years the Central Government had kept full control of the education of the German people. During the previous decade a huge problem for the country had been a lack of food, so official compulsory youth schemes had been established to stabilize German food production. Vocational education and training was given to boys and girls in order to get them working out on the land, thereby helping farmers to achieve maximum harvests, and most young people in Germany were expected to participate.

The repercussions of these youth schemes, however, had not reached *Kreis Grosses Werder* at that time. As an annexed 'Free State' much of the bureaucracy experienced by citizens residing in Germany took it's time filtering down to West Prussia which was, after all, mostly agricultural. The whole region was known as 'The Grain Supplier of Europe' and most of the children who lived there worked in the fields with their families anyhow. Ruth's summons was of an entirely different nature than forced farm labor; it was academic.

Since she was one of the top two girls in the *Tiegenort Schule*, the Headmaster was sanctioned to tell her she was one of the selected few chosen to be honored by the State. He explained that the local administrators had been authorized to seek out smart, gifted children and offer them the opportunity of a lifetime. Herr Hitler was so proud of these children he felt they represented all that was good about the Third Reich, and as a reward he was going to have them educated up to University standard at which time they could study to become the finest people that Germany had to offer the world. For this honor, they were to be sent to a very special school, where nothing would interfere with The Furor's ambitions for them.

"You should be flattered." The Headmaster told her. "You are being given a chance to excel at all the subjects you learn in this school and more; you will receive an education which is second to none, and as you are very talented in music, for that subject you will receive special tuition." The Headmaster added that a letter to that effect had been sent to Ruth's parents, and that if they agreed to her going, she would be leaving for the new school in two weeks' time.

As Ruth cycled home that day her mind was in turmoil. On one hand, the thought of studying her beloved music to a level that might help her become a professional was very tempting, and she was certainly excited to think that such an important opportunity – indeed, honor - had been presented to her. On the other hand, she wondered about her parents, Fritz and Augusta Lindenau. If she was going away to school, when would she get to see them?

Suddenly the enormity of moving away from home hit her and her thoughts began skittering this way and that. 'What about the ducks? Who would feed them and spend time with the baby ones the way she did? And what about her friend Brigitte, and her Grandmothers, her beloved Grandmothers – when would she be able to see them again?' She began pedaling furiously along the riverside path to her home on the bank of the *Tiege*, and by the time she reached the front door and flung herself inside the house, the tears were already pouring down her cheeks.

The moment she saw her mother standing across the room with a serious expression on her face and a folded piece of paper in her hand, she knew that the news had already arrived.

"Oh, *Mutti*, what am I going to do?" Ruth wailed. "Did you tell *Papa* about it? What does he think?" Her mother walked towards her and gave her a long hug. "Well, *Ruthchen*, it would be a wonderful opportunity for you. To be educated with all those clever children in such a place, and to be educated so fine; think how proud you would make your *Papa* and me."

Although the familiar smile on her mother's lips and her words of encouragement were genuine, Ruth noticed there was something behind the words which rang a little hollow, and her Mother's smile seemed more brave than delighted.

When her father came home that evening and the family sat around the supper table to eat their bread, cheese and *wurst*, they all felt as if a gigantic grey cloud was enveloping them; it was like having an elephant in the kitchen. Something of enormous import had happened to the family and each of them was emotionally torn apart while they wondered what to make of it.

Ruth and her mother spoke a little to each other on the subject, but Fritz Lindenau sat silently throughout most of the meal. He had delivered the letter from the Regional Office that morning. Seeing the postmark, he had been very curious as to why such an official-looking letter had been sent to him, but he had not had time to read it until his wife handed it over that evening; and it had quite taken the wind out of his sails.

Finally, after listening to his wife make brave comments to their daughter about her chance to be properly schooled, Fritz Lindenau spoke. "If you were not such a clever child, *Ruthchen*," he began with a wry smile, "we would not have to worry about you leaving us. But you *are* clever; and although your mother and I will miss you more than we can say we want what is best for you, and it seems that this fine education you are being promised is just that. It is what is best."

Fritz Lindenau was not a highly educated man. The height of his ambition had been to live and work in peace in his beloved village, raise a family with a wife at home and, in the future, have many grandchildren. His work was hard. In all weathers he rode on horseback with a big leather bag slung over his shoulder which sometimes weighed fifty pounds. In winter he had to cross a frozen river to deliver mail; and if his horse slipped and fell through the ice Fritz went down with it and returned home that evening with his heavy serge overcoat, frozen stiff and solid to his back. In summer he enjoyed his routine, plodding around the countryside to deliver mail and greeting everyone he met. Fritz was a man of few words. His wife ran the home and organized their lives and he was more than happy to let her do so.

In the past few years, though, since the German Army had invaded Poland, things had changed dramatically. His country was at war and everything that seemed safe and familiar to him was on the verge of deep uncertainty. His step brother-in-law, Otto, had pledged his allegiance to the Nazi Party at the start of the war, much against the opinions that Fritz and his wife held, and he was running his huge farming estate on the hard labor of prisoners-of-war. Fritz was surrounded at work and in the village by people he had always known to be good Christians who, one by one, began to lean towards the opinions of Adolph Hitler. Some of them voiced open hostility towards the Jewish people and others were turning a blind eye to the fact that thousands of prisoners were routinely taken in loaded trains to Stutthof, which was only fourteen kilometers away from where he lived, and put into a camp where, he had heard whispered, horrific things were happening.

He was beginning to hear rumors from colleagues at work and from some of the farmers he met while delivering the mail, that the German Forces were not always doing as well as they were being told on the radio. So far, thankfully, he had not been called to join the Army, but he had no idea if it might happen in the future; and if it did, maybe his youngest child would be safer and better off in a school full of children which their soldiers would be certain to protect.

After voicing his opinion, he looked in turn at his wife and daughter, who were both silently staring down at their supper plates, and after a long pause he spoke again. "I really think *Ruthchen* that you must do what the authorities say."

'That was it,' thought Ruth. 'This was not *Papa* and *Mutti's* choice. It is what they have been *told* will happen; and the letter asking for their agreement is nothing more than a token.' She looked at her mother, perhaps hoping to see her shake her head in disagreement with her husband, but Augusta Lindenau remained still, and silent.

After what seemed like several minutes, Augusta slowly raised her head and looked into the eyes of her daughter. The same brave smile Ruth had seen earlier was again on her mother's lips, but as Ruth returned her gaze, she felt a small jolt in her heart. 'The light in her eyes,' thought Ruth 'has died.' And suddenly she was afraid.

The next two weeks passed in a blur for the entire Lindenau family. Ruth went to school each day, but instead of dawdling home with her friends as she used to, sometimes going into their homes to talk and do her homework, now she hurried home on her bicycle to spend as much time as she could with her parents.

She soon confirmed her belief that her classmate, Helga Vogel, was the second girl in the school to be offered the chance to go away. Helga and she usually contended for first place in most of their schoolwork, so Ruth would have been very surprised if somebody else had been nominated.

Helga's parents, it seemed, were as conflicted as her own about the sudden opportunity put their daughter's way, so at least the two girls were able to commiserate with one another, discuss their situation and try to cheer each other up about leaving home.

With only two weeks to prepare for her departure and so much to do, the time passed swiftly. Augusta laundered and mended Ruth's clothes, and made sure she had everything she would need for a year away from home. The letter had stated that parents would be allowed to visit their children just once a year; and Ruth was growing so tall. Her mother was concerned she had warm clothes that fitted her properly when the perishing cold Polish winter arrived, and so Brigitte's mother helped Augusta alter Ruth's warmest skirts, jackets and dresses. The letter had also stated that the school would provide uniforms for the girls, but Augusta desperately needed to keep busy, and she wanted Ruth to have clothing to wear when the uniforms were not required, so clothing items that would soon be outgrown needed to be lengthened and let out.

Once the garments had been folded and carefully packed, and Ruth's favorite books and sheet music and her old rag doll were nestled amongst her clothing, the only remaining job was to say goodbye to her relatives. It was the hardest job of all. Her aunts and uncles and, especially, her grandparents were very close to her, but at the same time they were proud that she had been given such a special opportunity; so they gave her loving words of encouragement and cheer which helped to reinforce a small sense of excitement Ruth felt at the thought of all the special music studies she would soon be having.

It was a bittersweet day for the whole family when Ruth's father, full of pride and hope for his daughter's fine new education, loaded her trunk and boxes of personal possessions onto a horse-drawn cart, and lifted his little girl up to sit amongst them. He was in no hurry to flick the reins and get the old horse moving, but once Augusta had climbed up beside him there was nothing left to do except head for the *Tiegenort Bahnhof.*

Helga and her parents were already at the small station house when they arrived; all three of them sitting forlornly on a bench while they waited for the train. When Helga spotted Ruth, she jumped up and ran to greet her friend, looking visibly more cheerful now that she was not having to deal with her departure alone. The parents made small talk together for a few minutes while the girls carried their lighter bags to the edge of the train tracks, and then walked over to stand with them and wait for the train. In true German style, when the second hand on the station clock had almost reached the eleventh hour, the puffing and chugging sound of the train signaled its imminent arrival.

The train was bound for Poland, which had by then been commandeered by the German Army, and a city called *Tczew,* then known as *Dirschau,* and the destination of the girls was a *Landjahr Lage,* which roughly translated means "Retreat Camp," in a region named Bartenstein, about 90 miles further on. As the train pulled out of *Tiegenort,* with Ruth and Helga leaning out of the windows waving tearful goodbyes, neither they nor their parents could possibly have imagined how much time would elapse before they saw each other again.

The distance to *Dirschau* wasn't very long, about fifty kilometers, but the journey took about four hours because the train stopped at every little village and hamlet on the way. Ruth and Helga began to build up a good deal of tension and nervousness as the hours rolled by, feeling a growing sense of loss as they moved further and further away from their parents and their homes. Churning stomachs were not conducive to hunger so by midday, when they were usually famished, they looked at the folded cloth napkins containing their lunch and looked away, to stare again out of the train window.

The chunks of good dark bread, made that morning by Brigitte's father, topped with slices of smoked ham and packed for their lunch on the train by their mothers were left, untouched.

Instead, they watched the *Weichsel* river snaking its way into the distance, through fields of waving corn and oats, and lush green meadows where herds of dairy cows grazed, swishing their tails and disturbing swarms of insects trying to settle on their golden-brown backs in the hot mid-day sun. All they could think about was that the same river they saw was flowing through their village meadows and past their homes, where their parents were probably wandering about and feeling lost without them being there; thinking of their daughters traveling far, far away.

At one place where the train pulled in, a group of uniformed German soldiers boarded the train and demanded to see their papers. Helga had mislaid hers and was nervously searching in her bag when an officer standing next to her began yelling and berating her for being so slow. Fumbling around in all the bag's compartments, Helga finally produced the required documents; but she was tearful and shaking as she handed them over for inspection and was not able to regain her equilibrium until the train pulled into *Dirschau,* when a new kind of nervousness overcame her. Only another 90 miles; the last leg of the journey was about to begin.

CHAPTER THREE

The girls waited anxiously in *Dirschau* for a local train to come and transport them to Bartenstein near *Munster Walde,* the hamlet where their new school was located. They didn't have long to wait for in less than half-an-hour a shrill guard's whistle heralded the arrival of the train, and soon after they heard it puffing its way along the rails toward them, with fluffy white clouds of steam leading the way.

Several other young girls had boarded the train by the time Ruth and Helga were seated in a carriage. Some had arrived at *Dirschau* by horse and cart, while the rest had arrived on a train traveling from the opposite direction. It was apparent to Ruth that they were all headed for the same place; the quiet attitude and serious expressions of the new traveling companions belied any other explanation, and soon enough her speculation was proved to be correct.

When the train pulled into *Bartenstein* an hour later, and all the carriage doors were opened, every young female on the steaming, hissing train, eight in all, clambered down onto the platform. A couple of porters came to help unload their trunks and within a few short minutes, just like magic, two old men with beards, wearing worn moss green boiled-wool jackets and serge, khaki work-pants appeared from the back of the *Bahnhof* and started calling out, *"Landjahr Lage! Landjahr Lage! Wie viel maadchen fur das Landjahr Lage?" "How many girls for the Retreat Camp?"*

Suddenly, the platform became a hive of activity and noise while everyone called out to the newcomers and tried to identify their bags and trunks, which were now stacked up in piles by the entrance to the station office. The old men, who looked a bit like garden gnomes, were somewhat bent; but working on the land had obviously strengthened their muscles, for within a short space of time all the girls' belongings were loaded on to two farm carts. Each cart was harnessed to a farm horse, one chestnut the other a brown and white piebald; both patiently pawing the ground while grazing on a strip of grass outside the Railway Station entrance.

With their luggage in one cart, the eight nervous and exhausted young girls climbed into the other; glad that their journey was almost over and very anxious to arrive at their destination. One of the men, who introduced himself as Gunther Brehm, told them that the cart-ride to their school, about seven kilometers, would take about half-an-hour. The other man, who told them he was Frederick Brehm, Günter's brother, seemed anxious to get started. The afternoon was drawing to a close, and although the evenings were beginning to lengthen, he was concerned they arrive at the school before dark.

The roads around *Munster Walde* were basically country lanes lined with hedgerows and overhanging trees. Apart from an occasional small farmhouse set back from the road, nothing could be seen of a real village. The bumping and wobbling of the cart as its wheels struck stones and potholes in the road made the journey so uncomfortable that Ruth began to feel impatient to arrive at the school. After a couple of miles the hedgerows grew lower, eventually disappearing, and in the dwindling evening light the girls were able to see fields stretching for miles, some looking like seas of green, planted with leafy stalks of new corn and others lined with furrows, lying fallow, still waiting to be planted with crops.

They were in an area of working farms, Ruth thought, just like the fields around her own village, and the very notion of that made her feel a tiny bit more comfortable. The light had almost disappeared from the sky when suddenly the horses picked up speed and, looking up in surprise, Ruth saw in the distance a conspicuous building on the horizon. She knew immediately that she was seeing for the first time her school and her home for at least the next three years, and her heart seemed to leap into her throat. The very thought of it felt like a lifetime.

The dark silhouette of the house grew large and became quite striking as the carts approached it, and when Herr Brehm confirmed that it was their school the girls all murmured sounds of approval. It certainly looked like a beautiful place to live in. Named simply *Munster Walde,* the structure was known as a *Schloss,* or castle in German, but it did not have an appearance of the turreted granite and stone castles found in Britain and other parts of Europe. Rather, it looked like a grand country house of stately proportions, with a fenced garden surrounding its large grounds and a courtyard in front of the building. Certainly, it looked nothing like a Retreat Camp.

When the German Army had invaded Poland and taken over the property of *Munster Walde* two and a half years previously, it was used as a military post, but later, as larger more strategically favorable buildings were captured it was changed into its new capacity as a *Landjahr Lage,* a.k.a. converted school.

Once the gate was opened by Frederick, who led with the cart full of luggage, and the horses had clattered through and started off down the driveway, lights could already be seen coming on in some of the windows of the house. It was a long driveway, for by the time the carts had arrived at the stabling area at the rear of the house it had already turned dark and the outside lighting in the cobbled stable yard and around the perimeter of the house had been turned on.

Herr Brehm ushered the girls into the house through a back entrance which opened on to a hallway, down which the eight young travelers trooped until they arrived at a closed door. They looked around for Herr Brehm to come and open it for them, but he had already turned on his heel to go and assist his brother uncouple the horses from their burdensome loads and settle them in the stable for the night.

They all stood around uncertainly; none of them having the courage to make the first move and open the imposing door confronting them. A minute or two passed, and soon it was clear without a single word having been uttered who was being 'volunteered' to lead the group. A series of whispers and nudges between them had pushed the smallest girls to the back of the group and the bravest ones to the front, and Ruth, being the tallest, found herself front and center and so close to the door that her nose was almost touching it.

Although she was confident in her opinions, Ruth sometimes displayed an introverted exterior, but her height and direct green eyes belied that side of her nature and emphasized, rather, a look of self-assurance. To that end, the small group of girls who had been her traveling companions for much of the day had somehow decided that Ruth should be their spokesperson so, gathering her wits and her courage, she hesitantly raised a clenched fist and tapped her knuckles against the door.

For a moment all was silent, and Ruth was about to knock again when a muffled female voice was heard from within. It sounded a little impatient; as though the owner of it was tired of repeating the order she gave. "Hierein," the voice cried, with an accent on the last syllable, "hierein, hierein!" Come in, come in! Ruth clasped the brass doorknob and turned it, assuming correctly that nobody else was going to do so, and as the heavy door opened, she led the way inside.

An aroma of boiling vegetables met the girls' nostrils immediately the door opened, and stepping inside the room they found themselves in a large, warm kitchen with a red tiled floor, a huge pine table in the center and a large stove against the far wall, with an attached pipe which went far up the wall and disappeared through the ceiling.

The smell of the cooking vegetables was not particularly pleasant, but it was not bad enough to prevent the girls' mouths from watering as they suddenly realized how hungry they were. The feeling, however, didn't last long; all thoughts of food were soon dispelled when a severe-looking woman in her mid-fifties, with dark hair pulled into a bun on the back of her head and wearing a tailored white blouse and a long black skirt, rose from a chair in the corner, by the stove, and stepped towards them.

"Welcome, young ladies, welcome to *Munster Walde*." She said unsmilingly, "I am Fraulein Gerde Schmidt, one of the three instructors here. I am afraid you have already missed supper, but there is a little soup left over and some bread, and if you want to serve yourselves after I have shown you to your dormitory you have my permission to come back down here to eat it."

The girls all thanked her, and then introduced themselves one by one and told her where they came from. Strangely enough, it was the first time that Ruth and Helga had heard the other girls' names. All of them had been so nervous and wrapped up in their own thoughts on the journey, they hadn't even communicated that basic information to each other.

Fraulein Schmidt nodded in acknowledgement as each girl explained who she was and where she was from, and then led them through the kitchen to another door on the right-hand side of the room, which opened into a large square foyer with shining parquet floors. A wide hallway at one end led to the front door, and around the walls heavy closed doors held the secret as to which rooms lay behind them. A wide imposing staircase opposite the front door curved its way up through two levels to the top of the house.

Fraulein Schmidt paused for a moment in the center of the entrance

Hall, and turned toward the girls who were trooping along behind her. "Here," she said, raising her right arm and waving it in the direction of the doors, "are your classrooms. You will enter them and be seated at your desks each morning by eight o'clock. Breakfast is served in the dining room," she waved a hand in the direction of another closed door, "promptly at seven o'clock. If you are late for breakfast, you will go without. "Normally," she continued, "you will use the back staircase to go to your dormitory, but in this case as you are new arrivals, we will take the main one."

She turned quickly on her heel, strode across the floor to the foot of the stairs and without hesitating climbed them two at a time until she had reached the second floor at the top of the house, where she turned toward the stairs and waited for the girls to join her.

Not one of the girls was over fourteen years of age, yet some of them were breathless when they reached the top stair at such a pace. They would all soon learn what it meant to be really fit but on that evening, they remained oblivious, and that was good; for at least on this, their first night in *Munster Walde,* they deserved a good night's sleep after such a harrowing and emotional day.

All the doors on the top floor had brass numbers on them, except for one at the end of the corridor. Fraulein Schmidt indicated to them it was a bathroom which all the girls on that floor shared. She opened the door with a number three on it, and putting a finger to her lips indicating silence, she showed the girls inside.

It was difficult to see very much as the only light in the room was from the reflected light in the outside hallway from which they had come, and some filtered light through cracks in the shutters of two windows on the far wall, which allowed one of the outdoor lights to shine through.

The room was long and not very wide, and on first impressions it looked exactly like a sick room in a sanitarium. Spaced equally along each white wall were ten three-tiered bunk beds, all exactly facing each other, and except for a beige and brown carpet runner in the center of the floor between the beds, there was no color in the room at all.

A small bump, visible in several of the beds, indicated someone was sleeping there, but when the door had been opened no-one moved, no-one stirred, and no sound could be heard. It was almost too quiet, suspiciously so, and Fraulein Schmidt was clearly not easily fooled. "Girls," she said briskly, "here are your new room-mates. Please make them welcome."

"*Guten abend,*" *Good evening,* came back a sing-song chorus of voices, "*guten abend,* Fraulein Schmidt." The eight girls murmured their hellos in return, but Fraulein Schmidt did not think an acknowledgement was necessary. "Come," she said to Ruth and her companions, "follow me." She walked the length of the room towards the windows where a set of shelves and cupboards were built in each corner of the wall. "Here you will keep your belongings." She said. "Everything must be kept neat and tidy at all times or you will be punished."

She continued, "Each morning at five thirty you will be awakened by the school bell, when you must get up and take turns to wash your faces here." She indicated a wash basin on a pedestal between the two windows. "After washing you must make your beds. The girls here will show you how to do that in the morning, won't you, girls?" The last sentence, she called into the room, but no muffled reply came back as the words had sounded much more like an order than a question. "Twice a week you will take a shower in the bathroom down the hall. There are sixty-five of you altogether and the bathing schedule is posted on the bathroom wall."

With each new instruction, the girls silently nodded their assent. Ruth could see everyone's face now that they were standing by the windows where the weak shafts of light were coming in, and they didn't look very happy; in fact, they looked downright miserable. The big fancy house that had attracted their interest and attention as they approached it down the long, manicured driveway was rapidly beginning to feel more like a prison.

Chapter Four

By the time the girls had unpacked their belongings and placed them as neatly as they could in the twilit area of shelves and cupboards, no-one had a desire to go back down to the kitchen and try to figure out how to re-heat the soup and find spoons and bowls. So far, everything in their new residence had seemed far too intimidating and they were all quite happy to leave any new discoveries until the following morning.

While they unpacked, Helga and Ruth discovered their folded napkins containing lunch, which their mothers had made for them. Although the bread was getting stale and the edges of the ham had started to curl and harden, they shared their food with the rest of the girls, breaking it up into pieces so that everyone at least had a nibble of something to put in their empty stomachs.

The eight girls all crouched down to eat around the empty bunk beds which Ruth and Helga had selected, when a round little face peeked over at them from the top bunk and whispered, "Hello, I am Anna." They invited her to join them, and Anna didn't need to be asked twice. She scrambled down the lower two bunks immediately, delighted to be included in the prohibited activity which had already begun.

"Fraulein Schmidt would be very angry if she knew you were eating in here." Anna warned them earnestly, her large blue eyes wide open. "If she catches you we will all be punished, so hurry, and make sure you don't leave a trace of food anywhere. Fraulein Schmidt has eyes in the back of her head, I swear; and you won't want her to find any evidence when she does her daily inspection tomorrow."

Anna needn't have worried. Her new friends were hungry enough to eat up every crumb and then scavenge around for any dropped ones, even in the dark! When the last morsel of bread had been eaten and the girls were hungrier than ever, having awakened their digestive juices, they introduced themselves to Anna. Ruth, taking the initiative, began.

"It's nice to meet you, Anna, I am Ruth Lindenau from *Tiegenort*," she whispered, "and this is Helga, my classmate." "I am Berta Sommerfeld and this is my sister, Trudi." A freckle-faced girl of medium height for her age, with dark blonde wavy hair, had spoken. She nodded towards her sibling, another freckle-faced girl with slightly lighter blond wavy hair, who was so similar in appearance to her that they could have been mistaken for twins. The sisters must have been used to the misperception because Trudi added, "There is a year between us."

"I am Ingrid Wenzel," said a chubby girl with round rosy cheeks and a mischievous grin. Her heavily muffled voice parodied the whispering of the others and indicated that she might be fun to have around. "I'm Liesel," said another girl, with blue eyes and pale blonde braids, "Liesel Bauer." "And I am Mathilde Seligmann from *Marienburg*," piped up the smallest member of the group. She was a tiny girl with an impish face and dark curly hair, which was cut short and framed her face like the loose, round curls a small child might portray around a head on her first attempt at drawing a girl's portrait. "I am here with Bernadette Thoms," she added, taking the hand of a thin, bony girl sitting on the floor next to her. "Bernadette is afraid of being here, but I am not." She thrust her chin forward in a small gesture of defiance. "I am going to take care of her." Bernadette nodded meekly and smiled gratefully at her small defender. She was undoubtedly much taller than Mathild, but her face had a nervous worried look which probably made her vulnerable to being bullied. The rest of the group smiled sympathetically. Clearly, since they were all in the same boat, a tacit agreement was already forming between them that they would stick together and support each other in this new and somewhat intimidating environment.

Next morning, a loud clanging bell woke Ruth from a deep exhausted sleep. Even before she opened her eyes her heart sank as she remembered where she was, and she felt the prickle of tears behind her closed lids. The only thought that gave her a modicum of comfort was that she was not the only one. Sixty-five other girls lived in this house, and they were all in the same predicament.

She thought of her mother and father in *Tiegenort,* and how much they would be missing her when they awakened that morning, and the tears started up again. All around her the other girls in the room were scrambling out of their warm beds, some grumbling and some silent. Nowhere, Ruth thought, could she hear the sound of cheerful voices.

Helga, who had managed to acquire the bunk above hers, swung her legs over and climbed down to the floor via the edge of Ruth's bed. She crouched next to Ruth, who still lay silent under her warm quilt. "Come on Ruth," she said urgently, "we need to go and wash and then learn how the beds get made in here. Hurry or you will be in trouble before the day even begins!" Her wide-eyed anxious expression resonated with Ruth and she reluctantly pushed back the covers. "All right, I'm coming." She said, getting up. "Don't worry; I'll be finished in here before you!"

Walking over to the wash basin, Ruth waited in line for the girls ahead of her to finish splashing water on their faces and brushing their teeth; and as she lingered there, gazing at the floor, she realized that the windows were no longer shuttered. A fragile morning sunlight was streaming through the glass and casting pale yellow lines on the wooden parquet. There was something about the lines though. She looked directly at the windows and her heart missed a beat; both windows were protected with heavy iron bars.

A feeling almost like panic seized her suddenly, but as she looked around at the rest of the girls going about their morning chores and ablutions, seemingly without a care in the world, the sensation left her almost as quickly as it had come. Ruth was a very practical girl with a good deal of common sense, and she told herself she was being stupid. The bars were probably there to keep the girls safe at night, in case any of them walked in their sleep; she was at the school to get a fine education and to study her beloved music, and all these thoughts of being trapped had to be driven away.

She didn't have time to dwell on her thoughts. A woman's voice, calling out for all the new girls to come to the front of the dormitory, broke through the muted conversations in the room.

About fourteen girls ended up facing the woman to whom the voice belonged. The extra students must have arrived earlier in the day from another area. They all had the anxious look of newcomers; ready to learn and willing to please. The woman, who appeared to be in her mid-thirties, stood next to a large wicker basket with a lid and handles which she had pushed through the door, and was now unbuckling a leather fastener which held the lid secure.

"Good morning, girls," she said, "I am Inge Werner, one of your instructors." Her voice was quite friendly; not at all like that of Fraulein Schmidt. "Here are the clothes you will wear every day while you are here at *Munster Walde*. On weekdays you must wear the black skirts and white blouses; and on Sundays or when you are folk dancing, you will wear these." As she spoke, an old woman with a lined, weather-beaten face and wearing a long apron over her dress re-opened the door and turning around in the entrance she bent down and pulled a smaller wicker basket into the room. She set it down next to the large one and struggled to quickly open the buckle on its leather strap, but the woman appeared to be all fingers and thumbs. Inge stepped over to help her. "Thank you, Magd," she said irritably, "that will be all." The woman named Magd straightened herself with some difficulty and then, respectfully saying "Yes, Fraulein," she gave a series of small bows from her waist and she backed out of the room.

"These are your best dresses," Inge Werner raised the lid of the basket and pointed inside, "your dirndls. There are two colors, blue or pink with white flowers. I see we have some tall girls here." She said, eyeing Ruth and Bernadette. "And a small one," her gaze dropped to Mathild. "Choose the ones that fit you best and if necessary, we will have them altered. Your shoes are in the bottom of the large basket; they must be kept clean and shining at all times and you will find polishing equipment for that purpose in a side room off the back hallway to the kitchen.

That is all for now except for your hair. Those of you with long hair are required to part it in the middle, braid it and then coil the braids around your heads. Those with short hair must keep it short. No frivolous hair styles may be worn here at *Munster Walde*. Now, off you go. Select your clothes and get dressed, and then the rest of the students will show you how the beds must be made."

The girls all scurried over to the baskets and foraged inside to find skirts, dresses and shoes which fit them. They realized they needed to co-operate with each other for, if nothing else, they were now very hungry for breakfast. Ruth realized with a pang of regret that her mother need not have worried so much about altering her clothing and buying her new shoes. She was to have no choice about anything, including what she wore at this school, this *Landjahr Lage;* this *Munster Walde.*

Frauleins Schmidt and Werner had one other colleague. The new girls met her at breakfast and they all disliked her on sight. She was heavily built, with short brown wavy hair, a round, badly complexioned face sporting several chins, mean 'piggy' eyes, a squashed snout-like nose and a tight, round, cruel mouth. Her name was Hildegard Muller, and her attitude indicated she held a grudge against the world and thoroughly disliked everything and everyone in it. Save, perhaps, the people who had put her into the position of power in which she found herself.

Their instantaneous aversion to this woman, however, was not caused by her looks, but by the way she treated one of the new girls at breakfast. The food provided was a form of grits, which had been boiled in water until it took the form of a grey unappetizing-looking sticky lump, which was then dolloped on everyone's plate by the old woman, Magd, who also worked in the kitchen. The nervous girl, Bernadette, tried to eat her portion, but was unable to swallow more than a spoonful. Perhaps it was due to the fact that the child was scared out of her wits at the whole experience of being there, but once Fraulein Muller spotted Bernadette's full plate, she seemed to take it as a personal affront to the school cook. She began yelling across the room to the cowering child, telling her to eat her food immediately; but Bernadette simply hung her head and crouched over the table with a look of such forlorn unhappiness on her face that most people would have taken pity on her.

Little Mathild Seligmann, Bernadette's self-appointed protector who was sitting beside her, took Bernadette's hand and smiled at her encouragingly. Everyone had already been told not to speak during meals, but Mathild did her best to help her friend from incurring more of the instructor's wrath than was necessary. She squeezed Bernadette's hand and nodded towards the full plate. Unfortunately, her silent entreaty was too late. Fraulein Muller was already marching across the room to see to it that the food was eaten.

"Who do you think you are?" She yelled at the cowering Bernadette, "The Queen of Prussia?" Her voice dropped to a wheedling simper, "Do we want hot *brotchen* and eggs for our breakfast, then, or perhaps we would prefer pretzels with butter and marmalade?" And again, she began shouting, "Is our lowly cereal not good enough for you? Eat it at once, you ungrateful girl, at once!"

If Bernadette had been disposed towards making another attempt to finish her food at the beginning of Fraulein Muller's tirade, the last sentence which was spat directly in her face, put paid to any thoughts she may have had to make amends. She became so terrified that her whole body shook with fear, which unfortunately gave the instructor more fuel to propel the pleasure of her chastisement. Grabbing a handful of Bernadette's hair in her left hand and her spoon in the right, she pulled the child's head back, which forced her mouth to drop open, and shoveled one glutinous spoonful after another between her protesting lips.

Coughing and choking through her tears, Bernadette did her best to swallow, but a large amount of the cereal ended up in her lap and on the table in front of her. That situation, however, did not seem to bother the bullying instructor, who was simply using the moment to make a point to all the girls in her charge that none of them had *ever* better mess with her.

By the time breakfast was over, everyone was suitably sobered enough to be in a state of dreaded expectation as they filed into Fraulein Muller's classroom where, they had been informed, the majority of their first day would be spent. The instructor devoted the time to instilling a series of rules and regulations into the minds of the new girls. They discovered that lessons were split into four classes a day, with approximately fifteen students in each classroom. "Classes" consisted of everything from working in the fields and gardens around the property to cleaning the wooden floors of *Munster Walde* on their knees, with nail brushes, spirits and polishing cloths.

Some academic classes were promised, but they would all be dedicated to learning the new culture of Germany. Instruction would be given on the Third Reich as governed by the Nazi Party and lessons on the teachings of *Fuhrer und Reichskanzler* (Leader and Chancellor) Adolph Hitler, who had recently changed his title to *Fuhrer des Grossdeutschen Reichs* (Leader of the Great German Nation). These lessons were based on Hitler's concept of *Lebensraum,* or Living Space, an ideology which had been adopted by the Nazi Party and was aimed at legitimizing the war and expanding space for the German people.

In addition, the girls were informed there would be regular classes on the old German traditions, for which Ruth was utterly thankful. Singing, folk dancing and learning to play musical instruments was also part of the daily curriculum, and everyone was expected to participate. The Fuhrer insisted that taking pride in the great German culture should be uppermost in the minds of every student; and drilling them with traditional music, dancing and singing was, in his opinion, critical to instilling that pride.

At the end of the day, when the new girls were asked if they had any questions, Ruth was the only one with the courage to speak. *"Bitte,* Fraulein Muller," Please, Fraulein Muller, she enquired directly, "will we be learning mathematics and geography and history and science, as we were told before we came here?" Fraulein Muller cracked her face in a surprised grin. "You will learn only what I have informed you," she said disdainfully. "Some history and geography will, of course, be taught during your culture classes, but only as it pertains to Germany. Nothing else is important to you. There is only *one* thing that is important to remember, *Ein Volk; Ein Reich; Ein Fuhrer.* Repeat this before you go to sleep at night and when you wake up in the morning, so that you will never forget."

She began to dismiss the class, but Ruth wasn't finished. "And, *bitte,* Fraulein Muller." There was a low but audible intake of breath from some of the girls. "When will our parents be allowed to come and visit us here?" She asked. Fraulein Muller's response drove a pang of alarm into every young heart in the room. She simply sneered in disgust at the bold enquiry and turned on her heel to walk out of the door; Ruth's question, clearly, was not worth endorsing with an answer.

Chapter Five

Shortly after her arrival, one of the girls, Monika, confirmed to Ruth that *Munster Walde* was, indeed, just like a prison. To prove her point, when they were crossing the courtyard in front of the house one morning, Monika told her to look over at the all the windows in the building. Ruth was shocked to see that it wasn't only the dormitory; every window in the house was barred!

As the days passed and lessons progressed, all the new girls realized that their 'school' was very different from their expectations. The students who were already familiar with the strict regulations gave them dire warnings about breaking the rules; most of which concerned anything that involved a student attempting to be an individual. It was better, they were told, to do everything according to the system. Even if it meant something as innocuous as parting one's hair in the middle of one's head instead of being creative and trying to part it on one side or having no parting at all. Anything perceived by the three women who ran *Munster Walde* as being disobedient would be severely punished.

After her audacious questions to Fraulein Muller on the first day, Ruth quickly realized that the domineering woman watched her very closely while she went about the daily schedule. As she walked in and out of classrooms, sat in the dining room or entered the dormitory, the woman's piggy eyes seemed to be everywhere, watching her with an expectant squinting sneer, as though she was just waiting for an inevitable slip-up on Ruth's part. Ruth was convinced she was smart enough to avoid that happening, since she knew that any real blunder she made was destined to land her in a heap of trouble resulting in dire punishment; so she kept a low profile for a few days and waited for Fraulein Muller to set her sights on somebody else.

Within a few short days it required no persuasion for all the new students at *Munster Walde* to understand the consequences of forbidden actions, and by the end of the first week, they had pretty much experienced what life would be like for them on a day to day basis. First, the school was nothing like any they had experienced before. Large groups of students were sent out every day into the fields to work on the crops which were grown on the property. They were told that everything from gathering fruits and berries in spring and summer, to cutting and digging vegetables in the winter was part of their curriculum.

Cold days in that far-northern place were in the majority. When feet and fingers were aching with cold, and the very air they breathed escaped from their nostrils like wisps of smoke, foraging for potatoes in wet, muddy trenches with bent broken-handled forks was a nightmare. Sometimes, the effort of putting but one item into a basket felt like a small triumph, particularly when all they had to hack off the frozen stumps of cabbages was a blunt knife, or been provided with a rusty old spade to dig into the hard, icy ground for turnips. Within a week or two, they would notice a girl went missing. They discovered through whispering in the dormitories that the girl had been punished. Usually for a minor offence, like asking when she could write to her parents. The offending girl would be punished and told, sometimes at gunpoint, to stand in the courtyard in her nightwear, all night. If she protested, the so-called Instructors would strip her entirely, and still make her stay in the courtyard all night. Some of the more delicate girls couldn't take it. They died of frostbite and were never spoken of again. If anyone cried, or protested, or grieved for a friend, their punishment was severe, so in order to survive the girls slowly began to understand that feelings of any kind did not exist.

No matter how small or delicate the girl, or how much a full basket of vegetables weighed, it had to be carried across long field tracks to a horse-drawn cart, onto which it was loaded. Hours after starting the chore, when the baskets were full, they were then taken back to the house where the vegetables were removed and taken down to a storage cellar. From there, they were washed and prepared for cooking, usually by the students themselves, if that was the duty for the day. The fact that produce was grown, however, did not necessarily mean that it was fed to the students. Although they were occasionally given a thin soup made with turnips or potatoes and cabbage, most of the meals provided were made of the breakfast grits they encountered on their first day and were served up either runny or lumpy. The three female instructors and military personnel, who frequently visited *Munster Walde,* were the main recipients of food produced on the property, and they were never shy in making sure that the girls saw how much more appetizing their own meals were.

Cleaning the parquet flooring in *Munster Walde* was another part of the syllabus. All girls were required to keep the gleaming surface maintained on a regular basis, and it was not an easy matter. On their hands and knees, they were instructed to first clean the floor with small wire brushes dipped in alcohol to scrub off the dirt, after which they were required to go all over the floor again with oil and rags, rubbing and polishing to recover the shining, burnished beauty of the wood.

The large surface of the floor took many hours for two young girls to complete, and the fumes of the alcohol often made them nauseous; but no matter what, if the task wasn't completed within an assigned time, they were made to begin all over again. And they missed meals and bedtimes until the job was done.

It was fortunate for Ruth that an emphasis on music was upheld in the school because it helped her situation considerably. Her mood only lifted during music lessons, the single class which interested her; and because she was clearly talented and worked hard, it soon became clear to the instructors that she was a valuable part of that activity. Her talent soon began to shine through, and as she took her subject very seriously and worked well, she was almost immediately made conductor of the school choir.

It was extraordinary that each day, in the midst of all the tough treatment, music and dancing was an equally important facet of their studies. The bullying tactics used in the classroom and the relentless discipline while working in the fields, eating their food and even when they went to bed, stood out in strange contrast to a singing or dancing class, where they all had to portray light-hearted carefree attitudes. In a day consisting almost entirely of what could only feel like punishment, but which ended in music, the girls found their only little bit of salvation in a wilderness of senselessness.

It was, of course, impossible to stop all sociable contact between the girls. Some of them, the more friendly ones, found ways to communicate with one another quite quickly. While they were working in the fields there were long periods of time when they were not closely supervised, and if they kept their heads bent, they could have long conversations without anyone observing them. Any hopes they may have had to develop their new friendships, however, were soon dashed. "Making friendships," Fraulein Muller told them, "only leads to problems like petty jealousies and favoritism. Your attention must not to be taken up with such trifles." She added that only by learning well the lessons of German history and the new doctrines set out by the *Fuhrer,* would they be ready to help direct their country into its glorious future. The Fuhrer was depending upon them, and all the other children in privileged schools like theirs, to be perfect leaders. Their influence would eventually spread throughout Europe. They would hold high above their heads the *Bundesdienstflagge,* the German flag, and be the chief representatives of German ideals, and the rest of the world would follow them."

This was the closest clarification the girls were given as to the real reason for their 'education'. The sheer size of the plan was so vast and so far beyond their imaginations that very few of them were able to entirely comprehend the *Fuhrer's* intentions. Those who grasped the general purpose of the idea had a fleeting notion that they should be flattered at being chosen, but the feeling did not endure.

As a culture, the German people tended to follow rules, and as children, the girls had been taught since infancy to obey their parents and other adults in their lives; but equally, and especially as female children, they had been encouraged to be caring, affectionate and thoughtful. Their hard wiring was not reacting well to the present handling they were receiving at *Munster Walde,* where they were being re-programmed to forget all feelings of kindness, love and compassion. None of them had any choice but to obey the stringent and inflexible rules and to endure the harsh, callous treatment at the hands of their instructors, yet deep inside them the new message was not resonating. The majority of the girls wanted nothing more than to go back home to their families; even if it meant being exposed to the dangers of the war which was raging over their homeland. They had been told that the German Army was protecting them where they were, that they would be much less safe back in their homes; but their hearts held less concern for themselves than for their families, and to be separated from them at such a violent time in the world made the parting doubly hard to bear.

For Ruth, it was a living nightmare. She was fortunate to have experienced a happy, secure childhood with very little discipline. Her father was a quiet gentle man who worked hard and said little, preferring to leave his wife to take care of guiding their daughters; and her musical and singing talent had always ensured that she mostly enjoyed positive, if not spoiled, attention from her elders.

She felt a certain comfort in the fact that at least she now knew the *real* reason why she had been sent to *Munster Walde,* but the knowledge only fueled her resentment. 'These people have no right to take me away from my parents,' she thought, 'and they lied about it. I'm not being prepared for any University. All they want is to turn us into hard, cruel women, like Fraulein Muller. I'm being pushed into doing something I have no interest in doing, and I need to get away.'

Fraulein Muller's clarification of the reason everyone was there, certainly explained why the girls were not encouraged to be friends with one another. They were being made to put aside their own feelings for the sake of upcoming responsibilities. If, in the future, when they were instructed to influence groups of people towards a certain ideology, and some of those people opposed and tried to appeal to their better nature; there would *be* no better nature. It would have been forced out of them.

The appalling significance of Fraulein Muller's statement went mostly above the heads of the students. They basically only understood that they must not make special friendships with one another and that they must study and learn all there was to know about the teachings of their *Fuhrer,* Adolph Hitler. Ruth was not too bothered about the former rule; she had little concern or interest in the other girls except, perhaps, Helga, who was an old schoolmate though not a close friend. Ruth was used to being with Brigitte, who was stronger-willed than Ruth and was sometimes nasty to her, but Ruth admired her because Brigitte taught her wheedling tricks, and how to charm and then pull the wool over adults' eyes. After Brigitte, she liked being with her cousin, Hanschen, whose intellectual star was much dimmer than Ruth's, so she sparkled and shone alongside him. Ruth did not understand why anyone other than her mother should discipline her, and she deeply resented the fact that total strangers had that power.

She was so miserable and unhappy in the state of abandonment she felt that during most lessons she couldn't help herself, and more often than not would raise her hand to ask a question. Since most of them were related to her personal predicament, such as, had a letter arrived from her parents that week, the punishment was instant and automatic. Her instructor would bark immediately, "Kitchen duty! *Sofort!*" Immediately! And Ruth would leave the classroom, glowering with anger and frustration that she had once again been told nothing to ease her wretchedness.

As a talented singer, pianist and now conductor of the choir, Ruth slowly became aware of the fact that she was, in a subtle and intuitive way, playing a bizarre game of give and take with her instructors. No matter how many times she asked questions in class, and it was often, she began to notice that the only reprimand she received was kitchen duty, the least severe punishment of all. Party officials occasionally came to *Munster Walde* to see for themselves how well the children were being educated, and the fact that Ruth was an important part of the musical activities which, in turn, gave the school a good image, could have meant that the three supervisors might be going a little easier on her.

As this knowledge seeped into her sub-conscious Ruth used it to full effect, making sure that the choir she directed was a model of perfectly-schooled choristers which reflected an example of an efficient, faultlessly-run school; and although her constant questions brought no satisfaction, at least she found she was able to release some of her pent-up frustration by asking them.

The days turned into weeks, and the weeks into months, and her personal punishments remained the same, kitchen duty. Ruth managed to avoid other hazards which befell many of her fellow students, but when the punishment was a general one which applied to them all, she endured it with everyone. For example, the girls' dormitory was inspected daily, and each bed checked for uniformity and precise making. Top sheets had to be folded over the blankets to an exact measurement of millimeters, and then tucked tightly under the mattresses, and pillow positions all had to be the same. If a sheet was found to be a bit wrinkled or a pillow was not squarely in its requisite position, every bunk was stripped, the bedding thrown on the floor and every child was told to drop whatever they were doing and put the dormitory in its proper order.

In the area where the girls kept their belongings, each shelf was scrutinized daily for neatness. If a single item was misplaced, which meant not folded to an exact size or slightly hanging over the shelf, the whole stack of shelves was tipped over until the entire contents, everyone's possessions, emptied out onto the floor. Then, of course, each item had to be replaced correctly by its owner.

However well a child might have performed her lessons in a single day, no matter how much she might have shone during, for example, a recitation from a section of *"Mein Kampf,"* there was absolutely no favoritism for any of the students when general punishments were in order. If two girls were discovered by an instructor talking or, more correctly, whispering, after lights out, the entire dormitory was punished; and the punishment was instant and harsh. Spring or summer, winter or fall, they were all taken down to the courtyard and made to either march around it all night or stand absolutely still until the morning bell sounded.

Ruth experienced this punishment with her fellow students many times during the period she was there. If it was hot at night, which was often the case in that region during the summer, the girls had to march continuously around the courtyard wearing heavy clothes. They were forbidden to stop; no water was allowed and if one of the girls fell from exhaustion, she was yelled at until she struggled to her feet and continued marching. In winter, which could be brutal, the opposite punishment was administered. The girls were made to stand still wearing nothing but their flimsy nightclothes and experience what it felt like to get frostbite, which some of them did. Indeed, some of them died, though nothing was ever made of it.

The utter senselessness of the life she was now living started gnawing away at Ruth's sanity until her every waking moment was consumed with the same question; whether or not she could soon see her parents and beg them to try and take her back home, where she would be treated lovingly again. She was not interested in anything she was being taught, much less being forced to learn, and even the music classes began to hold little joy for her. During the first few months, music lessons had been the periods that sustained her and gave her the courage to get up in the morning and face each unpredictable day; but as time went on and only one supervised letter to her parents was allowed each month, her homesickness and deprivation of everything and everyone she was familiar with began to overwhelm her.

She learned in one letter from her mother that her father had been given orders to enlist. The news particularly distressed Ruth. The fact that she hadn't been able to say a proper goodbye to her father was bad enough, but as each day passed another cause for anxiety crossed her mind. The fact that the Army was now recruiting men of her father's age could mean that the war was not going so well for Germany; contact with her family was so limited, she began to have visions that she would never see her beloved *Papa* again. Desperate to know what was happening outside, she tried to be observant and keep her ears open for any news of the outside world, especially when she saw delivery men or local people talking to the three women who totally controlled her new way of life.

CHAPTER SIX

From time to time, military personnel and officers came to *Munster Walde.* Usually they came alone but occasionally they were accompanied by bureaucrats and local officials. For most of their visit they disappeared into one of the elegant living rooms in the house, which the students were forbidden to enter, but later, when the meetings were over, they could be seen crossing the courtyard to another part of the house where they were served lunch or dinner with the school's three instructors. Presumably, because *Munster Walde was one of the largest properties in the region, they* went there to plan top secret local strategic maneuvers, for during the entire time the meetings were conducted, and while they dined, uniformed soldiers were posted around the courtyard to guard the premises.

The girls were absolutely forbidden to fraternize with the visitors, but their presence alone brought a breath of fresh, outside air into the confines of the school, and each time they came to *Munster Walde* everyone became excited and anxious to catch a glimpse of them. The majority of girls were far too nervous to get close to the visitors, choosing rather to take peeks at them between the bars of the dormitory windows, but the first time Ruth saw them, she felt her first glimmer of hope in a long time. Several weeks went by before she saw them again; and again, a little chink of optimistic light switched on in her mind.

At the start of her stay in *Munster Walde,* the visits from the strangers had been on, perhaps, a four to six-week basis; but Ruth began to notice that after receiving the letter giving news of her father's enlistment, the meetings were becoming more frequent, about every two weeks. This was another reason to wonder how well the war was progressing, and it made her more nervous than ever about her family. 'Why did these officials keep coming to the school for planning talks?' Ruth asked herself. 'Something important must be happening outside. *I have* to find out!'

As she observed the usual pattern employed by the visitors when they entered the property, a germ of an idea started to form in her mind; an idea which she kept to herself. In any event, if she was caught the whole school would undoubtedly be made to pay but sharing her thoughts with somebody else could make the consequences even harsher.

She wasn't planning to do anything too stupid, but rules were rules and she already knew the kind of punishment they might all suffer if she was caught. The soldiers on guard duty around the courtyard looked quite young to her, and she was sure she looked grown-up enough to approach one of them and ask for news of the war. Ruth had a determination which was hard to shake, but once her plan was settled and her mind was made up, it still took a couple more visits from the visitors to finalize her scheme and put it into action.

It was easy for the students to recognize the days when visitors were expected, for several reasons. First, the day before, a great hurrying and scurrying about the rooms and hallways of the main building could be seen, while Magd and several students on cleaning duty dusted furniture, swept floors and polished brass. Next, a large bouquet of flowers and leaves was arranged in a huge ceramic container and placed on a round table in the entrance hall. And last, much to the secret amusement of the students, on the day of the visit the instructors became quite agitated, especially Fraulein Werner who was visibly nervous and excitable, running in and out of the kitchen to make sure that enough food was being prepared, and even impatiently snapping at her colleagues as she dreamed, perhaps, of having a quiet moment alone with one of the handsome officers who were about to cross *Munster Wald's* threshold.

The fact that their instructors were distracted when the visitors came was a huge bonus for Ruth, and she was determined to take full advantage of it. She planned to ask her usual question of Fraulein Muller on the morning of the next visit and, fervently hoped she would receive the usual kitchen duty as punishment. While the visitors ate lunch together with the instructors after their meeting, she would slip out of the kitchen to the back door and run around to the corner of the house where one of the soldiers would be on duty. Ruth knew that one of her jobs would be to take the vegetable peelings to a large compost heap in the garden after they had been prepared for the guests' lunch, so leaving the kitchen would not be difficult.

On the day she decided to implement her plan, she was surprisingly calm. Indeed Fraulein Werner, who was on duty in the dining room during breakfast appeared to be considerably more keyed up than Ruth. A faint flush brightened her normally sallow complexion, and she kept patting her hair and nervously looking over her shoulder to the door, as though she expected one of the officers in uniform to come marching in for breakfast. In view of their domineering characters, it was hard for the students to imagine any of the three instructors being attracted to men, much less that men would be interested in them; but Fraulein Werner, being the youngest and certainly least aggressive, was without doubt behaving that morning as though she had set her sights on something other than disciplining the group of students surrounding her. If it were not the case, at least half of the nauseating-looking grits served to everyone for breakfast would not have been quietly returned to the kitchen.

Later, while the army officers conducted their meeting in the drawing-room, Ruth sat in class and prepared herself to ask Fraulein Muller a question. When it was framed in her mind, she raised her hand, her nerves still under control. She had asked so many questions before that she was getting used to it. The only difference this time was that she decided to ask something new; something which, hopefully, would virtually guarantee that she would be sent to the kitchen. "Bitte, Fraulein Muller," she began, when the teacher lifted her chin enquiringly in Ruth's direction, "why do our soldiers and officials from town come here more than they used to? And why," she added for good measure, "are we not given the same vegetables they eat here when they visit?" As Ruth left the classroom, banished to the kitchen, Fraulein Muller berated everyone that they were not deserving of such luxuries, and never would be for as long as they resided in *Munster Walde*. Strangely enough, with the arrival of the officers the younger Fraulein Muller's tirade sounded more like an admonishment than her usual tyrannical outbursts.

Everything went to plan while Ruth worked in the kitchen. Once she had collected all the vegetable peelings into a large copper bowl, she scraped on top of them the large amount of discarded breakfast grits which, incidentally, Magd could not fathom why they had not been eaten, she hurried outside to the compost heap. Seeing no sign of anyone, she emptied the bowl and returned to the house, where she positioned herself close to the back door with her back to the wall. It was bitterly cold outside, and most people tried to stay indoors on days such as this, but if somebody did abruptly come into view, Ruth had the empty bowl as evidence that she had been performing a task and could return quickly to the door and re-enter the house; but so far the whole area was clear. Looking around in all directions she cautiously moved along the wall to the end of the building and taking a deep breath she peeped around the corner. By her reckoning, and according to past procedure, the soldier on duty should be at the far end, standing guard; but she saw nobody in the expected place. Her heart skipped a beat as she felt a surge of disappointment, but an instant later she saw a little cloud of steam in the air and a soldier's uniformed arm appeared half-way around the corner of the building. The steam was escaping from his nostrils as he breathed the cold air. Clearly, he was moving around in the restricted area of his guard-duty trying to keep warm.

Ruth relaxed a little and, surprised by her own audacity, she immediately began moving again, along the wall towards him. This was the riskiest part of the plan for her because she was now a long way from the back door of the house and significantly more exposed. She was so occupied looking behind her as she progressed along the wall that she almost bumped into the soldier before seeing him! First, she heard a slight noise, and looking down she saw a black marching boot. Again, her heart skipped a beat, but as she looked up into the very handsome face of a young, blonde soldier, she had the prudence to raise her forefinger to her lips and gaze pleadingly into his wide, ice-blue eyes.

The young man was clearly shaken; but not only by the close presence of the young woman who had crept up on him unawares. The fact that she was a budding beauty of exquisite proportions could not be ignored by him. She was almost his height, with braided, copper-colored hair and the greenest eyes he had ever seen. He struggled quickly to regain his equilibrium and show her that he had an important job to perform, but the young woman had already started talking and, really, standing there with an empty bowl in her hand and the look of an innocent child on her face, he couldn't imagine that she was there to harm anyone. He managed to muster a frown as she spoke. "Bitte, mien Herr," Ruth said hurriedly in a voice barely audible to him, "I am a student here and we are strictly forbidden to associate with the visitors and soldiers. Can you please stand and face the courtyard while I speak to you?" The young soldier was reluctant to move his eyes from her face, but he saw how frightened she looked as she constantly glanced over her shoulder, so he slowly turned his back to her. "Danke shone, mien Herr." He heard her voice behind him, a little louder now. Perhaps she was relieved that he had not arrested her. The voice continued a little breathlessly, "Can you please tell me what is happening in the war? My father went into the army and I am very worried about him, and I'm also worried about my mother who is all alone now. I need to be with her. How are our soldiers doing? Do you think the war will end soon?" With the last question Ruth put her hand gently on the young man's back, clad in a belted grey field jacket, and looked pleadingly at his shaved blonde hair, cut into an immaculate straight line below the back of his slate-grey felt field cap.

Only a few moments passed before he replied, but it felt like an age. Ruth realized that his voice sounded quite young, but it was soft and kind and she knew as he began to talk that he was trying to be considerate. "It would not be fair of me, Fraulein, to tell you something I don't know." he began. "I can tell you that the Generals are concerned about the Red Army's advance; but at the same time, we are told that we can easily defeat them. It's all a matter of strategy, they say. We foot soldiers just do as we are bid and go where we are told to go. I, too, would like to be back home in Berlin. I'm sorry, but I can tell you nothing more."

It was enough. Ruth knew that he was not lying, and she had been out of bounds for long enough. "Thank you, mien Herr," she said, unable to keep a disappointed pang from her voice; and turning her back to him she glanced quickly around to make sure that nobody was coming into view. Günter or Frederick Brehm might easily appear on their way to the stables, though it was unlikely because albeit in the rear of the property, the cobbled yard with its' housing for the horses was situated on the opposite side of the building.

She was again in luck; all seemed quiet in every direction. In spite of the lack of real news, things had gone so well for her that she sensed a small feeling of elation, even excitement, in the pit of her stomach. She began to slither her way back along the side wall to the end, and by the time she reached it the feeling had increased.

She knew before she turned her head that she could not go around the corner without giving a backward glance. The young soldier was standing perfectly still, watching her. Their eyes met down the length of the wall and for a second or two, held. Ruth was frozen to the spot, but when he raised his hand very slightly in a gesture of farewell, the small motion shocked her into action and she scuttled along, close to the wall, until she reached the back door.

As she stumbled into the corridor her heart was beating fast and she felt breathless. Something had happened that she wanted to remember; to savor and learn from. The feeling was beyond anything she had felt before, and she was going to keep it to herself because she didn't yet understand it, but it felt like power.

Somehow, in spite of the fact that her head was spinning, she found her way back into the kitchen, where Magd was so busy preparing lunch for the visitors that she barely noticed Ruth's arrival. Several other students had been given kitchen duty to help cook and wait on the honored guests, and everyone was focused on the task in hand. Ruth joined in the fray and hugged her new knowledge to herself.

That night, as she lay in her bunk bed, she had a chance to properly evaluate the events of the day. Now that the anticipation of her deed was over and the adrenalin had subsided, rather than experiencing a sense of accomplishment she was left with a hollow feeling in the pit of her stomach. Her daring escapade achieved, she realized how harsh the consequences could have been had she been caught; and although the excitement of her meeting with the handsome young soldier remained with her, the lack of news he was able to relate disappointed her immensely.

Indeed, all the students were anxious to know how the war was progressing, and Ruth knew that. Even more importantly, they all wanted to know when their parents would be allowed to visit.

As time went on a strange camaraderie grew between the girls, but more often than not it only showed itself in their eyes. If someone was punished, her fellow students were forbidden to defend or protect her. Sympathy was absolutely prohibited, and everyone soon found out that crying was a useless and futile act.

Clearly, they were all being toughened up and trained to tolerate rough treatment and conditions. Kindness and pity were forbidden values. It was as though loyalty, consideration and reliability were being crushed out of them; and worst of all, talking about their parents and families was *verboten*. The only time it was impressed upon them to be faithful, honest and devoted was when the tutors insisted, they must always demonstrate those qualities to the *Fuhrer and the Third Reich*.

The *Fuhrer's* reason for emphasizing artistic classes on young people had been made crystal clear to them, but all the girls cared about was that it was the only time in their day when they felt a tremor of enjoyment and pleasure coursing through their young, pubescent bodies. A time when they could remove their work clothes and uniforms and slip on their pretty dirndl dresses for a couple of hours, and pretend they were back at home with the local village boys, dancing in a *Fest*.

CHAPTER SEVEN

After months of depression, thoughts of home became so constant in Ruth's mind that they began to engulf her every waking moment; then one day she discovered that rather than depress her, the childhood memories fortified her resolve and gave her courage and a stronger determination to return home, no matter what.

She thought often about a dear old man with a long, grey beard and sparkling eyes from Tiegenort, Herr Klinger. He had fought in the First World War and suffered from severe injuries to his legs, which caused him constant pain. In spite of that he always had a kind word for everyone, never complaining but always passing on his words of kindness, compassion and wisdom. All the village children referred to him as Oopah, Grandpa, and they loved him because he showed a deep interest in every child and was brilliant at firing up their imaginations.

No matter how many children he saw as he hobbled down Hauptstrasse leaning heavily on his gnarled wooden walking cane, he would stop by each one of them and pass the time of day. How were their parents? How were they doing in school? Had they seen the waterlilies growing on the Tieg? Did they know that three of the dairy cows up at Herr Becker's farm had given birth to beautiful calves? Oopah Klinger always had something interesting to tell them, a little bit of local news to report.

Herr Klinger's motives were as pure as the driven snow that settled around Tiegenort's cobbled Main Street in winter. His own wife had died in childbirth along with his little baby daughter a quarter century before, and to help alleviate his great loss he had spent his life paying attention to all the children who crossed his path. Especially in these times of such turmoil he did his best to give the children something pleasant to think about. He told them tales of fairies and goblins living in caves in Germany, where precious jewels covered the floors and sparkled on every wall; and how when a stork came and nested on the chimneys and rooftops in the village it meant good luck. It meant that soon a new baby would be born in that house, bringing joy and happiness to the whole family. But one day in late December he told such a tall story that only the older children were able to truly understand him.

Ruth smiled as she recalled Oopah Klinger's best story ever. It made its way like wildfire around all the children in the village until early one snowy morning the old man found himself surrounded in his garden by such a large hoard of excited squawking, jumping and laughing children that he became quite overwhelmed. He sat down on a wooden stool on his doorstep and begged them all to calm down so he could understand what they wanted. "Oopah! Oopah! Is it true that you know Santa Claus? Tell us, please tell us!" "Now where did you get that piece of information children?" The old man demanded. "I cannot imagine you heard such a thing!" Little Ralphie Muller raised his arm and hopped up and down so he could be seen above the crowd of children. "I overheard Herr Kruger the other day," he shouted excitedly. "I was with mother in the Bakery buying our brotchen and he told his customers there were no cookies to be had in the store, so please not to ask for them." "Oh, really?" Said Oopah Klinger, thoughtfully, stroking his beard and pasting an innocent expression on his weather-beaten face. "And what reason did Herr Kruger give for the lack of sweet treats, mein kind?" The children hushed in order to hear the answer. "He whispered to his customers," squealed Ralphie, "that you, Oopah, that you had bought every cookie in the store! He whispered to the ladies thinking I wouldn't hear, but," proudly lifting his chin, "I was able to hear everything he said." "And what reason did he give that I would do such a foolish thing as that?" Quizzed Oopah, scratching his beard as though the answer might very well come from within the thick layers of grey and white hair. "Well, he noticed that I had overheard him, and he became flustered and said that you were friends with Santa Claus and you were going to give Santa the cookies and ask him to remember and come visit our village on Weinachten, Christmas." "Indeed, indeed," said Oopah, a smile creasing the bridge of his bulbous nose and lighting up his bright blue eyes, "well

I do happen to have met Santa Claus, it's true, but there is one little problem to overcome before he can promise to come all this way to visit our little village." The children waited in rapt attention; knowing exactly what the little problem was but not daring to ask. Twenty innocent little faces looked at the old man, eyes wide and expectant. The boys began shuffling their feet while the girls poked them and hissed them to wait and stay still. Oopah nodded sagely, "You know what I'm going to tell you, don't you, you little rascals? The important and only thing which will remind Santa to visit our village is if he is absolutely certain that all of you, I said all of you, are very good and very well behaved. If one child breaks this rule then Santa will have to bypass Tiegenort; and because I have my eyes everywhere in this village, Santa has asked me to report to him on the morning before Christmas."

Suffice it to say that every child in the village was helpful and cooperative that year. Butter wouldn't have melted in their mouths! And on Christmas morning, to their surprise, along with the modest number of gifts each child found in their stockings, a little net bag in the toe, contained a tangerine, a handful of almonds and four sweet, delicious cookies!

One day in the classroom when a particularly long list of items on the Third Reich had to be memorized, Ruth's mind again started wandering back home to Tiegenort and the classroom in the village school she had so loved attending.

Suddenly, as she began wishing that someone from home would just come and fetch her, just walk her out of the Munster Walde classroom and take her back to her family, a memory of something that happened when she was six years old flooded her mind and she began to smile.

She was sitting at the back of the schoolroom early one morning, next to her cousin, Steven, when the classroom door burst open. Everyone looked up in astonishment to see an elderly woman dressed in long skirts and a bonnet enter, walk vigorously across the room and stop at the desk of the teacher, Herr Klinger.

The intruder was Anna Lindenau, Ruth and Steven's grandmother, and rather than being embarrassed in front of the class the two cousins were simply alert and curious as to why their adored relative had paid the school a visit.

They didn't have long to wait for an answer, for Anna Lindenau began to speak before Herr Klinger had recovered his breath and composure. "Good morning, Herr Klinger." She said, "And what a beautiful morning it is indeed." As she spoke, she took Herr Klinger by the arm. "Come," she coaxed, tugging at his arm to prize him away from his desk, "come to the window with me and take a look outside."

Herr Klinger raised his elbow to fend off the enthusiastic little lady, but she would have none of it and hung on as if her life depended on getting the reluctant schoolmaster to the window. With all his students looking on in astonishment and, no doubt, wondering who would win this battle of wills playing out between their revered master and the spirited old lady, Herr Klinger decided that discretion was the better part of valor. His attitude suddenly changed and he strode willingly, albeit slowly, across his classroom, with Frau Lindenau still tenaciously holding his arm, to see what all the fuss was about.

If Herr Klinger had imagined that the lady wanted to point out something unusual to him, like two boys scrapping in the schoolyard or a stray herd of cows wandering across the school property, he was sadly mistaken. Nothing remarkable could be seen anywhere.

The children had all turned around in their chairs and were straining to see what amazing sight could be seen out of the window, but they, also, were destined to be disappointed; it just looked to them like any other summer day, beautiful to be sure, but simply another summer day.

"Now look outside, Her Klinger." Frau Lindenau crowed enthusiastically. "Isn't this the most glorious-looking June day you have ever seen? Look at the blue sky and the fluffy white clouds. And see the fields filled with corn and poppies in the distance, and . . .," as she uttered the last few words, she let go her grip on Herr Klinger's arm and opened the window, "and listen, Herr Klinger, listen to the larks singing with joy above the meadows!"

Herr Klinger nodded his head in astonished agreement, his popping eyes and the bewildered questioning look on his scholarly features plainly stated that he was waiting for more. Frau Lindenau did not let him down. Looking around the classroom, her eagle eyes alighted on her grandchildren, and she walked over to them, stood between their chairs and took a hand of each child.

"I am here, Herr Klinger," she said determinedly, "to take my grandchildren out for the day. It is almost a sin for these young people to be sitting here inside the school when they could be out, learning about nature. You can do what you want with the rest of the children in your class, but I intend to teach my grandchildren all about nature today, Herr Klinger, and I will not take no for an answer."

Frau Lindenau then turned on her heel, with Ruth and Steven firmly in tow, and bidding Herr Klinger a polite "Good Day", she marched her grandchildren out of the classroom and into the glorious sunshine, where they all walked with a grand spring in their step to the Tiegenort Railway Station.

Their destination was the seaside town of Stutthof, where they spent a day they would never, ever forget. All the way there, on the train, Grandmother Lindenau pointed out the wonders of nature to the children. The entire area was known as "The Bread Bowl of Europe" because so many valuable grains were grown there, and the sight of endless fields of yellow wheat competing for the sunlight with an equal amount of bright red poppies was a sight to behold.

While she was still in raptures over the sight of the poppies, the scenery changed to fields of barley splashed all over with the brilliant blue of cornflowers. Again, Frau Lindenau was transported into a similar state of enthusiasm, which only changed when she pointed out to the children a marvelous piece of architecture as the train chugged past an ancient church.

As they approached the coast, the sight of the ocean produced such an ecstatic sound of joy from the elderly lady that Ruth and Steven, who were by then thoroughly pumped up with excitement, thought they might burst if the train didn't stop soon and let them out to begin their magical day.

Ruth never forgot the details of that visit to the seaside; and more importantly she learned a lesson of courage from her grandmother. That amazing lady had no problem at all in confronting the schoolmaster and demanding that her grandchildren be released from lessons to enjoy with her the pursuit of nature and pure pleasure.

CHAPTER EIGHT

One morning, after Ruth and her new group had been at the school for about a week, they were all instructed to go to the nurse's office where they were told to take a pill. The nurse, Frau Meyer, a dark-haired woman with a ruddy complexion, whiskered pimples on her chin and cheeks and hairy forearms, informed them that the pill would keep them fit and healthy and free of aches and pains. Refusing to take it, even if it had crossed their minds, was not an option; especially since Frau Meyer put the small white pill in their mouths and watched each one of them swallow it down with a full glass of water.

The pill was administered regularly, but several weeks went by before the girls noticed that something was happening to their bodies. It began slowly. Ruth noticed one day in her reflection in the bathroom mirror that her face seemed puffy. It had been a hot day so she put it down to the fact that she had been working in the fields and might have got too much sun; but several days later the bloated look remained.

One night after lights-out, she tapped above her head on the base of Helga's bunkbed to signal she needed to talk. After a few creaks and scrapes Helga's face appeared, her hair hanging down like fronds of curly seaweed until it almost touched Ruth's pillow.

Since one of the three female guards at the school could walk in unannounced at any time, the girls had developed a kind of sign language to minimize speaking. Helga opened her eyes wide in inquiry to open the conversation, and the upside-down expression looked so funny to Ruth that she burst into a paroxysm of uncontrollable laughter.

Helga's wide-eyed expression immediately turned into one of horror, which snapped Ruth out of her unruly performance for a moment – at least, long enough to stuff a handful of sheets into her mouth when she realized how much noise she was making.

When she recalled why she had wanted to talk to Helga in the first place, however, she collected herself pretty quickly. Pulling the damp bed linens from her now silent mouth, she faced Helga and pointed an index finger to her cheek while raising her eyebrows questioningly. Helga frowned and shook her head, indicating she had not understood, so Ruth squirmed across to the edge of her bunk and put her mouth close to Helga's ear.

"Do you think my face is looking different?" Ruth asked, in the quietest whisper she could manage. Helga nodded yes, without hesitation, and then she whispered back "And mine is too. Look, I have two small chins." It was true. Ruth had been so worried about her own problem that she hadn't even noticed that Helga was beginning to look different as well. The fact that her friend felt she was in the same boat comforted Ruth somewhat, but she was still very anxious to understand the occurrence; perhaps even more so, now that both of them were experiencing the same phenomenon.

"Why do you think this is happening?" whispered Ruth, but Helga shook her head in bewilderment. "I don't know," she said quietly, "and I don't like it. Something bad is happening to us but I don't know what it is."

They agreed to ask Monika, their new friend, when they had a chance to talk to her. Monika had been there longer than most of the other girls and she seemed to know more about the goings on in *Munster Walde* than anyone else. The opportunity came sooner than they could have hoped for. Next day they were scheduled to share the bathroom with a group of girls which included Monika, and as bathing time was largely unsupervised, they were able to huddle Monica into a corner of the steamy, green-tiled washing area to raise their concerns over their appearance.

Monika, as they had hoped, understood immediately what they were talking about. "It's the pills." She said knowingly. "That bitch of a nurse is making us take pills to stop our periods. They don't want to have the fuss of all us girls having stomach cramps and headaches, which mean that we cannot work in the fields, so they stop our monthly cycles altogether; but the pills make us retain water and we become bloated."

Ruth and Helga listened in astonishment and Ruth's eyes filled with tears. "I wondered why I had skipped my period last week," she said, "but I thought it was because of all the stress of leaving home." "Oh, no," Monika shook her head sagely, "take a look at Mathild Seligmann. She is swelling up like a little balloon, and all you girls who just arrived will begin to do the same soon enough. Haven't you noticed how everyone here is sort of big looking? It isn't caused by muscles that we are developing from all the hard work in the fields; it's bloating."

No matter how unhappy she was and whatever the three bullying women did or said to her, Ruth made a decision to follow the rules and be a good student; while at the same time vowing to do her best to find out why she and all the other girls were virtually imprisoned at *Munster Walde,* and why they were being made to follow an impossible set of regulations which made absolutely no sense. Her resolution to 'play the game' was not too difficult as she took her studies, especially the music, seriously; but her new-found courage made her equally determined to speak up when she felt something was unjust.

She found the courage somehow to ask questions on a regular basis in the classroom; 'How was the war going?' 'Was Germany winning?' 'How could they know if their parents were safe?' 'What if their parents were killed – how would they find out?' She soon discovered that asking anything at all resulted in the same answer; 'Fraulein Lindenau, you are assigned to kitchen duty.' And Ruth would leave the class and go the kitchen where she would be given pots to scrub or potatoes to peel, or any other unpleasant job that the cook and her assistant did not want to do.

Kitchen punishment was far preferable to Ruth than the alternative, which was being sent to stand in a corner all day and to go without food and drink. It wasn't so much the lack of nourishment that bothered her as her inability to stand still all day. Ruth was an energetic person and having to maintain an inactive position gave her time to think, and then to dwell, on the situation she was in. She would end up feeling so angry and frustrated that the only thing she could do to regain her equilibrium was to recall an incident from her childhood in *Tiegenort,* which kept her focused on the happy times in her life.

Ruth was not the only one who was anxious to know what was happening in the outside world. All the students were. Other than the progress of the war they especially wanted to be given news from their families, but the information they gleaned amounted to nothing. Any letters they received were intercepted and screened, and opportunities to talk to outsiders were few and far between. Other than the occasional workmen hired to fix broken pipes in the plumbing system, or the local blacksmith paying a visit if a horse lost a shoe, contact with the outside world was non-existent.

One day, however, when Ruth had yet another kitchen duty punishment, she became aware that another chance to see outsiders was each week early on Monday mornings, when tradesmen from the village came to deliver flour and meat. She soon understood when to expect these deliveries, and if she or one or two other girls could manage to finish breakfast early enough on Mondays, they would hurry down the corridor to the kitchen and dart out of the shadows when a tradesman approached, to ask him for news of the war.

Several girls were willing to try and pry information out of the unsuspecting tradesmen, but it was critical that nobody was suspected, so they had to find legitimate reasons for being in the area of the kitchen and its entrance hallway. Little Matilde Seligmann was full of ideas, many of which were adopted.

Too many girls rushing off in the same direction would raise suspicion, so it was decided that at the most only two should leave the dining room at one time. Mostly, a pair of friends would help the kitchen staff carry dirty dishes back to the kitchen, and they would try to exit through the back door into the hallway when deliveries were being made. To allay the regularity of that habit, someone would occasionally need to run to the toilet, and fortunately there was one in the back hallway. Sometimes a couple of girls would be assigned to work in the garden on that particular day, and they would exit through the back doorway instead of the front; and occasionally somebody would actually have kitchen duty or punishment, which made the whole exercise much easier.

Either way, every week one or two girls tried to glean news of the outside world; and all news, whether good, bad or non-existent, traveled from student to student like wildfire. As girls will, they were not averse to using some flattering ploy or another to gain the information they sought. Sometimes they offered to hold open the kitchen door for a puffing and panting butcher delivering baskets of meat; or if the miller delivering sacks of flour was seen staggering back and forth to the kitchen, they would run to help him carry his burdens, each grabbing a bottom corner of the sack to lift a little weight off his load.

"How is the war going, Herr Muller," they would ask, "are we winning?" Or, *"Bitte, Herr Metzger,* what was happening last week when we heard the sound of planes flying over for most of the night? Were they our planes or English ones? We cannot tell the difference between the sounds they make."

More often than not they were greeted with blank stares and negative head shaking. It seemed that whatever was going on in the outside world, no-one in the *Dorf of Munster Walde* was aware of it. Either that or, most likely, delivery people had been cautioned to say nothing to the girls if questions were asked of them. It was very disappointing, but the girls never gave up. For the entire time they were in the school they tried every way they could think of to get information; however small the detail, however old the news.

The girls became resigned to the hard, physical work, the relentless instruction and indoctrination on the *Reich* and the senseless punishments they received. They now understood fully that the harsh treatment being administered was indeed an unrelenting technique to toughen them up for their adulthood.

Although very little information was given them, when a small hint was dropped here and there by the three instructors the smartest girls in the group were able to ascertain that much was going to be expected of them when they 'Graduated'. It was certainly obvious that the most talented individuals in the entire population of smart young women at the school were being weeded out and given extra attention.

They had been in *Munster Walde* for several months when the entire school was told they were going on a hike. "Simply put," Fraulein Muller informed them, "you are being put to the test. We need to see what you are made of. We will all be hiking to the nearby forest and beyond, covering a distance of one hundred kilometers. The hike will take four days; two days to get there and two days to return, and during these days you will learn and understand the meaning of survival.

In fact, when everyone set out it seemed just like a normal walking trip. Each girl wore sturdy leather shoes with studs in the soles, serge walking shorts, buttoned blouses and a khaki green sweater. On their backs they carried a pack holding a metal box which contained black bread and a rolled blanket; and hooked to a leather belt around their waists, a metal canister contained about one liter of water. It was early in the morning when the group headed out. They had been rudely awakened at 4:00 AM when the raucous, strident sound of a thick wooden stick being rattled around inside a metal bowl pierced the silence of their dark dormitory, followed by the sour voice of Fraulein Muller. "Get used to this noise, *mädchen;* it is what you will hear in the morning while we are away from school. The only bells in the countryside are the ones you will hear tied around the necks of cows."

Everyone scrambled to get dressed and make their beds before going bleary-eyed down to breakfast, where they were given a bowl of the usual cold, lumpy grey cereal which had, without doubt, been made the day before. It was a question of either eat or go hungry for the day, so most of the girls had the good sense to gulp down at least a portion of the sticky dollop in front of them before hurrying to the hallway to pull on their boots and pick up their packs; from whence they headed into the courtyard where they had been told to assemble at 4:50 AM sharp.

It was a morning in early September. The previous day had been hot and the warmth of it still lingered in the early morning air as everyone stood around and waited for the signal to set off. To be occupied with something different, a new experience, had triggered an air of excitement amongst some of the girls, and they were eager to begin the day. Just the thought of walking in the countryside and getting away from the constricted confinement in Munster Walde lifted their spirits. It was a heady feeling which drifted down the large group of girls, and most of them were looking forward to the change of pace.

CHAPTER NINE

On the stroke of 5 o'clock, the entire school of sixty five girls began their walk down the long driveway of *Munster Walde* and out into the surrounding farmland. In spite of her lingering suspicions that the four day hike was not going to be like a vacation, Ruth's spirits were ready to be uplifted; and as several of the other girls, including Helga, were smiling and almost jaunty, she relaxed her guard a little and briskly told herself to make the best of the beautiful day which promised itself on the far horizon.

By the time the girls had walked down the narrow country road beyond the school gates and begun walking on stone-laden pathways between fields of ripening grain, dawn was breaking. The twittering of birds was suddenly heard everywhere, and as the countryside awoke the sun appeared on the skyline, obliterating the previously discernible line between field and sky in a brilliant, dazzling burst of joy. It was so beautiful that for an instant Ruth felt breathless; and then, in the strengthening light a lark rose out of its nest in the field right next to where she was walking, and soared into the early morning sky, where it began a song of such sweetness and clarity that it was almost heart-breaking.

Ruth unexpectedly found she was crying. The silent tears came from nowhere, blocking her vision and pouring down her cheeks to the ground. Helga, who was walking alongside her, suddenly realized that Ruth had stumbled on a rock in the path so grabbed her arm and turned to look at her. She was amazed to see that her friend was in tears, but

Ruth shook her head and indicated that she was alright. Helga nodded; a sympathetic expression on her face. She was responsive enough to know that although her talented friend Ruth managed to find courage at the most unlikely moments, she was also sensitive and emotional.

The trek through the farmlands to the forest took longer than the girls had expected. The glorious sun which had risen earlier that day was now burning hot and relentless, apart from occasional times when small fluffy clouds sailed along and obliterated it for a few minutes.

By noon, when the sun was at its hottest, the long gaggle of sixty five girls had slowed down considerably. They were now walking in single file, strung unevenly along a narrow path between two fields. The stronger ones were in the lead, following Hildegard Muller and Gerde Schmidt, who strode ahead as though a pack of Rottweilers was chasing them. Inge Werner walked with the smaller and weaker girls in back of the group, who were having a hard time keeping up with the rest.

Inge Werner, the youngest of the three instructors, was a little less aggressive than her colleagues, therefore, one might have imagined that being in the back of the line would be a more pleasant place to be walking; but Inge was completely dominated by Hildegard Muller and the pressure was constantly upon her to be harsh and unyielding. Her continuous cries of *"Schnell! Schnell mach!"* – "Be quick! Hurry up!" were intimidating enough to the smaller girls to be taken very seriously, and they stumbled along as quickly as their little legs could go.

Everyone was tired, hungry and thirsty, when they finally reached a meadow of lush green grass dotted with yellow and white wildflowers, and the sense of relief they all felt when they were given orders to stop was quite overwhelming. Hildegard Muller stepped into the field and raised a long pole with a small German flag attached to it above her head and began waving it; which was the signal they had all been waiting for. It took a few minutes for everyone to reach the meadow, and when they arrived the first thing they did was to lie down in the long green grass and try to cool off.

The feeling of blissful rest did not last long; Fraulein Muller blew a shrill whistle to command the girls' attention. "Don't get too comfortable." she said, "We are resting only for twenty minutes. We have thirty more kilometers to walk before stopping for the night, and I warn you now, do not drink too much water; what you are carrying must last you for two days."

The announcement completely dismayed some of the girls! They had already been drinking from the metal canisters on their belts and had no idea how much of the precious liquid remained. The instruction was clearly delivered deliberately late on the hike and was intended to intimidate.

Suddenly, in one fell swoop, spirits which had been raised by the change of routine and the beautiful morning plummeted back to zero. Reality set back in immediately and even curbed the appetites of the more nervous girls in the group, who looked uneasily at the bread and ham they had started to eat and put it quickly back in its metal container. If the water was rationed, they reasoned, then surely the food must be as well.

The hungry girls, who hadn't given much thought to anything except the gnawing feelings in their stomachs, noticed soon enough what was happening around them, and one by one, albeit reluctantly, they stopped wolfing down their precious lunch and tucked what was left of it back in their boxes for future consumption.

~ ~ ~ ~ ~

When the flag was waved exactly twenty minutes later, signaling everyone to scramble to their feet and begin walking, the entire mood of the day had shifted. The exercise no longer felt like a good hike but a march, and the animated chatter of the girls from the morning had turned into occasional whispered comments and hasty signals of facial expression.

Ruth lapsed into a speed which was fast enough to keep up with the average-paced walkers in the group. She was still hungry, having just taken a couple of bites of her bread and a small slice of ham, but instead of dwelling on her hunger she switched her mind, as she often did now, to pleasant thoughts and memories. She remembered another time she had been hungry and a slow smile crept to her lips.

If she could have talked to Helga and told her the story she would have, because poor Helga was hungry having eaten even less than Ruth; but since developing friendships with individuals was frowned upon, excessive talking to one person was considered to be cultivating a friendship. In any event, Helga might not truly understand the importance of her companion's childhood recollection, so Ruth kept her sweet memory to herself.

It was early in the morning and she and Brigitte were lying in the grass on top of the dam. They were seven and eight years old, and they were thrilled with excitement over a new discovery. An enormous patch of violets had appeared overnight it seemed, all over their favorite spot in the village. They couldn't recall ever seeing them before. Perhaps the previous Springs had been too cold for the flowers to bloom, and before that they had been too young to be up on the dam alone together.

They eyed each other with smug delight, absolutely convinced that no-one else in *Tiegenort* could possibly know about their wonderful find. They sat in the grass for hours looking at the purple clumps of flowers, jealously guarding them. They kept busy picking daisies and making yards and yards of daisy chains, and they plucked wide grasses, putting them to their lips between their thumbs and blowing shrill sounds across the river. And all the while they busied themselves, they continually moved their attention from the tasks at hand to raise their eyes and check that the carpet of violets was still there; that it was not a dream or a figment of their imagination.

By late afternoon they suddenly realized how hungry they were. The bell in the church spire had been ringing the hours all day long, but the girls had only just begun paying attention to it. It rang five times. Lunch time had been hours ago, and a painful rumbling in their stomachs was reminding them that they had skipped it. Lunch was their main meal of the day. At four o'clock the adults stopped for *kaffee* and *kucken* and the children had milk and cake, but Ruth and Brigitte had missed that as well. Supper was later in the day when their fathers came home from work, and they didn't think they could wait that long. There was no point in running home and interrupting their mothers' activities. Both girls knew their mothers well enough to realize they would be making the evening's meal by now and would simply tell their daughters that if playing was more important than eating, they would just have to wait.

Ruth was all but ready to accept the inevitable, but a glint in Brigitte's eyes told her that her friend was not. Brigitte might have been a year younger than Ruth but she was an only child and, like Ruth, used to getting her own way. While Ruth could be plucky when she was pushed or affronted, Brigitte had a gutsy spirited streak in her which could sometimes turn mean; though most of the time she and Ruth got along well together. She pursed her lips and squeezed her eyelids tightly together as she thought the problem through, and minutes later she began to smile.

"I know what we can do to get something to eat." She said delightedly, "It's simple!" "What?" Said Ruth, knowing they couldn't go to Brigitte's father's bakery as he would be busy making dough in preparation for the next day's bread, and a golden rule existed that at that time of day his daughter must not interrupt him.

"We will buy something!" Brigitte said triumphantly. "Oh yes?" retorted Ruth, "And where," she added impatiently, "will we get the money?" "We will use our violets;" replied Brigitte, "we will pick them and sell them."

Within five minutes each girl held a large posy; and scrambling down the grassy slope of the dam they headed for *Landstrasse* where they separated and walked up the pathways of the first two houses at the top of the street. Boldly knocking on the front doors, they waited for the ladies of the houses to answer, and before long their patience was rewarded.

Two sweet little girls selling the first violets of spring for a few coins each was an easy sell, and a few minutes later with the spoils of their transaction clutched in their hands and smiles as wide as the River *Tieg*, Ruth and Brigitte ran helter-skelter over the cobbles to the store owned by Brigitte's uncle, the *Metzgerei*.

It was past five o'clock and the store was already closed but Brigitte's aunt and uncle lived on the premises, besides which, Brigitte knew how to twist her *Tante* Ursula around her little finger. Tapping on the glass door of the store with one of the coins in her hand, Brigitte, whose legs were shorter than Ruth's, was still panting and out of breath from the race down the street when her curious aunt stepped through a door at the rear of the store and came to see who was making all the noise. Her eyes opened in surprise when she saw the two young friends, but she obliged immediately and let them in.

"Oh, Tante Ursula," Brigitte wailed, putting up quite a performance and rubbing her tummy as she spoke, "we are sooooo… hungry, and you are the only one we can ask. Can we please have a piece of wurst? Look, we have money to pay for it!" And she held up her clenched hand and opened it up, revealing the paltry few *pfennigs* sitting in the middle of her palm. Her aunt smiled, greatly amused at the entreaty and went behind the counter. "Well, mädchen," she said lightly, taking into account Ruth's open hand along with that of her niece, "you don't have quite enough to pay for a slice each but I shall give you some anyhow." As she spoke, she pulled a length of wurst from under a protective glass cover and cut off two large slices. "Just don't tell your mothers that I fed you before supper," she chided them, "and make sure you are home before dark!"

The girls were overjoyed! A simple idea to sell violets for food had paid off big-time; they would do this again. They walked a few steps down the street before sitting down together on the curb, where they munched happily on their purchased wurst. No food in their young lives had ever tasted better!

It was mid-afternoon when her day-dream came to an end, and Ruth still had a smile on her face. The hunger she felt earlier had gone, but replacing it were aching feet, sore limbs and a thirst that demanded to be quenched. The afternoon had hosted a relentlessly hot sun with very little shade and the exposed parts of her hands, legs and face were burning like little furnaces.

Helga and all the girls around her were stumbling slightly in their haste to keep pace with the girls up ahead of the group with Fraulein Muller, and they too had burned-looking skin. For the first time in her life Ruth was grateful for the fact that she was taller than her peers and had less of a problem covering distance than they did; but the heat had affected them all, and they were desperate to sip some of the water in their flasks.

Monika, who had kept up with the group of walkers around Ruth whispered to Helga that if she couldn't have a drink soon she would faint, but Helga shook her head. "I know. I feel the same," she said, "we all do; but let us try and go a little further or there will be nothing left for tonight and nothing for tomorrow. We have at least another twenty kilometers to go before we can stop for the night." Monika moaned a little in reply, but as the person with most knowledge of their ruthless instructors, she knew that Helga was correct and plucked up her courage enough to let Helga know she agreed.

She strode on with her friends with her chin in the air and a look of determination on her face, when suddenly in the distance she saw a line of trees and knew that God above was watching them. "Look, look," she said quietly, "the forest is ahead. Now we will have some shade!"

It was clear to everyone when they raised their eyes from the stony path that the girls ahead had already seen the trees on the horizon, for they appeared to be hurrying, almost sprinting towards the blessed sight. An invisible ripple of energy coursed down the line of sixty five stragglers and fifteen minutes later the girls in the lead stumbled thankfully into the dappled shade of the forest; followed in short order by the rest of them.

Chapter Ten

As the girls walked deeper into the forest, the heavenly, welcoming shade helped to cool them down and soothe their spirits. Huge pine trees, or *Tannenbaum,* that had been growing toward the sky for decades and clamoring with each other for space and the light above, had entirely obliterated the sun below and created a twilit haven for summertime walkers.

The path underneath the girls' feet was thickly strewn with pine needles, making it smooth and unobstructed; and the clumps of fern, mounds of moss, tinkling streams and pine-scented air all around them created a fairy tale vision of familiarity and expectancy. If Hansel and Gretel had suddenly appeared on the path, nobody would have been surprised.

Unfortunately, Fraulein Muller had other plans in mind than loitering around in the cool forest. She told the girls that if they wanted to relieve themselves, they should quickly go into the woods to do so, and that she would give everyone ten minutes before starting out again.

The forest was not huge, just a few kilometers across, but the distance to its outer edge was long enough to allow the scorching sun to have cooled down a little by the time the girls reached it. They gazed with relief at the waning afternoon light over the fields, which stretched way into the distance, and hoped that their brief sojourn under the trees had fortified them for the final stretch of the day.

The countryside was beautiful in this region, and although the girls were tired and thirsty, they enjoyed seeing the beautiful old churches and stone mills, built hundreds of years before, which dotted the landscape. An hour passed, and then two, by which time all their good intentions about conserving water began to disappear. One by one, canisters were unclipped from belts and raised greedily to dry lips. Oh, the exquisite joy! To feel the cool liquid nectar in their parched throats! The moment was worth almost anything. There was almost a spring in their step as they arrived at an area of lush wetlands abounding with wildfowl, which noisily announced their presence as they dived into the marshy waters to catch little fish, and flapped up into the tall grasses to go after insects; squawking and quacking noisily at feathered companions who had the temerity to try and steal their hard-earned spoils.

Villages and farms seemed closer together in this part of the world, and as the sun started to sink towards the fields and the light diminished, Fraulein Muller began looking around for a barn which would be large enough to house them all for the night. When everyone realized what she was doing they all began to look. Exhaustion was setting in fast; the band of sixty five young ramblers had covered fifty kilometers that day and they could hardly wait to get some rest.

A small village surrounded by farms could be seen in the distance, and as the group approached it several suitable-looking accommodations appeared on the landscape. One farm in particular looked appropriate to Ruth and Helga. They nudged each other and pointed towards a large barn in the distance, set right next to an old stone farmhouse with ivy growing up its walls, but they were too distrustful of Fraulein Muller to tell her about it; she was quite likely to deliberately choose another place because they had suggested it. Ruth and Helga kept quiet and kept walking, knowing full well that Fraulein Muller was the kind of person who would make everyone walk on for as long as it took until she found a place that *she* liked.

Fortunately, the girls' ploy worked! Without signaling or saying a word to anyone, Fraulein Muller turned abruptly off the country lane upon which they were walking, climbed over a stile into a field, and headed for the farmhouse that Ruth and Helga had seen.

It was a lovely old farm. A windmill turned lazily in the distance, several horses grazed near the house and a herd of cows crowded together by the gate in a corner of the field in which they walked; no doubt waiting for the farmer to come and take them to the dairy for milking.

As the girls approached the gate, which opened on to a stone pathway leading up to the house, the cows refused to move. They turned their docile gazes directly on the group of strangers, chewing peacefully on mouthfuls of grass, and then they turned away. A large number of people arriving in their field and crowding around them neither impressed nor concerned the bovine ruminants. They were interested only in the task at hand; and that was to go with the farmer and unload their heavy udders of the milk they had been carrying around all day.

Fraulein Muller began waving her long pole around the heads of two or three of the cows, hoping they would part from the rest of the group and make a pathway wide enough for her to sprint through to the gate; but when the flag started to flap at the end of the pole and went a little too close to the large brown eyes of the creatures, they set up a mini-stampede of panic which resulted in driving the herd even closer together.

The girls all backed off a little and waited to see what their instructors would decide to do. It wasn't often that something got the better of the tyrants in charge of them; and although their expressions belied nothing, each girl in the group was secretly amused, if not gleeful, to see all three women in a quandary of indecision.

As luck would have it, after several minutes passed a door was heard slamming in the distance, and a man with a black and white collie running beside him appeared around the corner of the barn. The cows were immediately restless, and began mooing and bellowing in expectation, while the farmer called soothingly out to the herd to confirm that he was on his way. When he reached the gate and saw almost seventy women in his field, gathered in a group near his cows, his eyes almost popped out of his head. "What do you all think you are doing in my field, disturbing my animals?" He yelled, his face turning red. "If it isn't soldiers tramping all over my land it's girl scouts! Ruining my ..."

Fraulein Muller quickly regained her composure, and moving aggressively forward a few steps she barked at him, "Stop! Stop! I must come and speak with you at once!" No doubt those words resonated with the farmer. He knew the sound of an official voice when he heard it, and he stopped shouting immediately. Opening the gate to let his herd through, he called out to the collie "Go! Petra, go!" And she immediately leapt, barking, into the field, where she dodged between the legs of the anxious cows and ushered them all through the gate and up to the barn. In next to no time, the entire herd had vacated the field and was comfortably settled into the cobbled yard outside the dairy.

Fraulein Muller signaled everyone to stay where they were and walked up to the farmer who was leaning on the gate, waiting for her to reach him. While talking in a low voice, she pulled a piece of paper out of her knapsack and handed it to him. Even from a distance, her stance looked threatening. The farmer shook his head as she spoke, and after a few minutes he nodded toward the girls and turned around to point at the barn, at which point they understood that the transaction had passed. A sense of enormous relief spread over the group of girls. At last they could rest.

The barn was large and cool. It had been split into two separate areas; half of it was used for storing feed and the other half for housing the dairy herd. The section allocated for the girls was already about a third filled with fresh bales of hay for the winter feeding of the cattle. A few bales which had been left over from the previous year were stacked up in the far corner of the barn and the farmer, who introduced himself to everyone as Rudolph Knapp, took a knife from a leather sheath attached to his belt and walking over to the older bales he bent down and cut the strings tying them together.

His face was grim and inhospitable when he looked up. "You can scatter these over the floor to sleep on," he said, "and in the morning I will leave a churn of milk for you by the back door of the farmhouse. I wish you all a good night." And with that he was gone.

Fraulein Schmidt, in the far corner of the barn, was already laying a red cloth over a bale of hay and pulling food and drink from a leather bag. "Right girls," called out Fraulein Muller, as she sat down with her colleagues to eat a very substantial-looking supper of ham, hard-boiled eggs, tomatoes and bread, "start spreading the hay over the floor and then unpack your blankets and find a place to lie down. This is your dormitory for the night."

The girls set down their knapsacks and began strewing piles of fragrant hay alongside the barn walls. It took a while to achieve a depth of comfort between the stone floor and the top of the hay, but by the time it was done, everyone was ready to drop!

Nobody cared about their three callous instructors, who were now making quite a show of enjoying their supper; tiredness had overcome hunger. In fact, every single student could hardly wait to sink down into the warm, fragrant hay and sleep forever. Fraulein Muller watched them all with a mean smirk on her face. "Don't expect a long sleep;" she said, "in the morning we have the same distance to walk again. Departure time tomorrow will be five o'clock, just as it was this morning." Within minutes, the entire group of girls was sound asleep, and the occasional mooing of a cow in the connecting barn disturbed none of them.

Next day, just as she had promised, Freulein Muller woke everyone to the rude noise of a wooden stick being banged on metal. A deep groaning sound began to accompany the wake-up call as sixty five young women tried moving their sore aching joints into a sitting-up position. It was a signal of success for their spiteful instructor, who yelled at everyone to stand up immediately, and it was with considerable effort that the girls complied.

In the next-door barn a commotion of moos, impatient stamping of hooves on the stone floor and banging into buckets, indicated that their fellow barn-mates had also arisen and were already in the process of being milked. This was good, because the meager bits of stale bread and cheese left over in the girls' knapsacks did little to diminish their hunger pangs but, true to his word, Farmer Knapp had left the promised churn of milk for everyone, and the still warm, rich, freshness of it helped to satisfy their needs.

Starting out on that morning was one of the hardest things to do that anyone had yet experienced. To walk fifty kilometers in one day was bad enough, but to face the same grueling exercise on the following day was highly intimidating, not to say frightening, for the majority of the girls who, after all, were barely out of childhood.

An old galvanized tub holding rainwater in the yard outside the barn was the only means available to freshen up, and Hildegard Muller was quick to let her charges know that sneaking the water into their drinking flasks was a punishable offense. She also pointed out that although the cows used the same water for drinking, it was perfectly all right for the girls to clean up in it by splashing the water on their dusty hands and faces.

It was a bedraggled line of still exhausted children who re-traced their steps across the field on that second day. Within a half-hour of starting out the smaller ones were whimpering with pain from the blisters on their feet, incurred from the day before; and when the stronger girls offered to help by carrying their knapsacks or supporting their arms, they were forbidden absolutely.

Yelling loudly down the line, to ensure that everyone could hear her, Gerde Schmidt screwed up her red face into such a tight scowl that her piggy eyes all but disappeared into the folds of flesh pushed up by her cheeks, "You young women have to learn about discipline and about suffering!" She screeched. "When we are in pain we must soldier on for the sake of the mission. It is our duty to *never* allow our personal feelings to interfere with the task at hand; never! Now all of you get moving!"

The group struggled on, but before an hour was up the weaker girls had fallen to the back of the line and were soon lagging several hundred yards behind. As the morning wore on the sun began to shine hot overhead, and some of the girls stumbled and fell when perspiration blinded them from seeing large stones on the path. The heat was palpable; it shimmered in the dusty air over the stubble of already harvested fields and lay heavily on the drooping heads of parched cornflowers scattered all over the countryside.

Ruth felt the familiar sense of injustice bubble to the top of her consciousness. She knew there was nothing she could say; indeed she had already proved to herself several times that speaking up only got her in hot water and could even cause trouble for the others; but she deliberately slowed her walking pace down a notch or two and very soon all the girls in the leading group followed suit.

The change of pace was subtle, but it was enough to allow the weaker ones to close the gap between them a little. Ruth knew that as soon as their tough instructors, striding out in front, realized what was happening they would all be whipped back into shape; but it was worth taking the risk for a while, and they all managed to walk two or three kilometers in that way until fate stepped in and slowed the whole group down.

Suddenly, one of the girls behind let out a frightened yell and crumpled to the ground wailing in pain. Her legs had literally given way. Freulein Muller and her colleagues turned casually around to see what all the noise was about and would have ignored the situation and carried on once they ascertained it was only another student making a big fuss, but the cries of pain sounded particularly intense on this occasion. Hildegard Muller, being far less heavy and more surefooted than Gerde Schmidt, decided to investigate and sprinted to the back of the line of girls from where the wailing noise could be heard.

Little Anna Stein was the one on the ground, and it was not like her to create a scene. She had recently been made to cut two long rows of cabbages, which amounted to about eight barrow loads, on her own, as punishment for being caught whispering in class; and she had done it almost defiantly without raising a whimper.

Hildegard Muller shooed everyone away from the distressed Anna, who lay moaning on the ground, and crouched down to investigate the cause of the problem. Anna's knees were badly grazed and bloody from her fall, as were the palms of both her hands, but clearly something else was the cause of her predicament. One, by one, Fraulein Muller took hold of Anna's feet and raised her legs in the air, but nothing seemed to be amiss with her hip mobility. Then she squeezed and prodded Anna's thighs and calves, which produced an enormous cry of pain from the little girl. Both legs were in the grip of a severe cramp which held her, writhing, on the pathway, and no amount of massage and rubbing appeared to help.

The heat of the day and lack of fluid had obviously contributed to Anna's problem, but Hildegard Muller did nothing to alleviate it. Instead she rubbed Anna's leg muscles harder, yelling "Shut up, you stupid little bitch, and get up." "Get up!" She cried again, grabbing Anna under her arms and pulling her to her feet. "Now, move! Move!"

Anna's legs buckled under her body, but continuing to hold her up, Fraulein Muller instructed the two girls standing closest to her to grab an arm each and walk Anna until her cramp wore off. "Drag her, if necessary," she said callously "I will not allow a little thing like this to delay us any further. We have thirty five more kilometers to go before we stop for the night.

Like it or not, the situation with Anna slowed the group down considerably, especially since one of the girls holding her up was Liesel Bauer, who was rather a delicate girl at the best of times, but now she had huge blisters on both heels, which slowed her walk down to a limp.

As the morning wore on and noontime came and went, several other girls developed blisters and became affected by the heat. They were all longing to stop and have a drink, but their three instructors strode on as though they were completely oblivious to the large group of distraught girls in their charge. Every once in a while Inge Werner, who had moved up to the front of the line with the other two instructors, turned around to see what progress everyone was making, but as soon as one of the other women spotted her they dug her hard in the ribs and pointed ahead, signifying she must pay attention to the path in front and ignore the struggles of their charges.

Little Ingrid Wenzel, who was the chubby member of the group amongst the younger ones, was a shining star who drew everyone to her side. Even the older girls were fascinated by her. If anyone was going to make a joke about their present circumstances it would be Ingrid. Her sense of humor had saved many a girl from despair during their stay in *Munster Walde*, and although she always had something positive to say to the others, she was adamantly against all the things they were being taught in class, calling it propaganda and the viewpoint of a deluded mass of people. Ingrid was clearly one of the most interesting girls in the entire group. For a young girl who was not quite fourteen she had already formed strong opinions which differed greatly from the 'education' she was receiving.

When she spoke of her aversion to the prevailing politics in her homeland, she exhibited such a strong and unwavering sense of anger that it stood in stark contrast to her outwardly cheery and optimistic attitude towards life. Many girls were drawn to her, asking her to expand more on her thoughts of what their country was doing, but a much larger group were almost afraid to listen when she spoke. It wasn't that they disagreed with her so much as the fact that they knew so little and were not equipped with enough information to have an intelligent conversation. A strong sense of national pride had long been instilled into the minds of their parents, who had told them that what was now happening in the world was for the good of Germany and its people; and as young children, who were they to disagree?

The fascination with Ingrid extended to more than her opinions of the war. When she had the chance, she told the girls about the town her parents came from, where she was conceived; where fairies lived in caves and precious stones and minerals could be found. The girls couldn't understand why anyone would want to leave such a magical place, but when they voiced their opinions Ingrid told them about the terrible lack of food there – even worse than what they were now experiencing in *Munster Walde.*

Ingrid had most definitely lost weight since arriving there, but her stature was still something of an encumbrance for her, slowing her down and causing her to breathe faster than the rest of them. Yet Ingrid walked cheerfully on and always had a positive comment for everyone within earshot.

Ingrid was the progeny of two people who truly felt she was a gift from God, and they were determined to raise her with a desire to learn all she could, think for herself and make her own decisions. Having suffered greatly from hunger in their lives, when Ingrid was born, an undernourished, pathetic little scrap of human life, they had taken one look at her and made a pact that no matter how much they might have to deprive themselves, their child would live and flourish.

Ingrid was, without doubt, a clever child who was quick to learn and form intelligent opinions about the subject she was taught. Able to think independently without just accepting information, her questioning mind didn't shirk from seeking out the truth. She had a natural talent for music and a beautiful, sparkling voice which matched her dainty stature and optimistic personality. She was not, however, worthy material for the teachings at *Munster Walde.* Ingrid's parents had been in their forties when she was born, and they had been through enough pain and heartache caused by the First World War to make them detest the subsequent schemes and plans of Adolph Hitler and his followers.

Since sitting on her father's knee as a tiny child and hearing his story about how long he and her mother had waited for her to come to them; and then, later, listening to her mother talking about her life in another town in Germany, far away, where Ingrid's brother was born and later buried, and where her two grandmothers and mother had almost starved to death while all their husbands were fighting and dying in a useless, hopeless war. Ingrid's parents had given her no illusions about the narcotic of national pride, which was now, again, being drummed into the ears of the German people. Much as they loved their country, they yearned more for peace and safety, and a chance to be happy whilst living out the remaining years of their lives with their beloved daughter.

CHAPTER ELEVEN

When she was snatched, as it were, from the little school she attended in Saalfeld, Ingrid's parents were grief-stricken. It was as though their daughter had died. The great irony being that they had done their best to give their daughter a broad education and now that she was the shining star in her school, Hitler had deprived them of their beloved daughter.

Ingrid connected with Ruth very soon after arriving in Munster Walde and she spent their private snatched moments to talk telling Ruth all about her parents and her life in Saalfeld, a small town in the Thuringia region of Germany. Nobody except Ruth knew that as a newborn baby born into poverty, Ingrid had almost died. Her parents, Peter and Hannah, came from Saalfeld, and they were among the many thousands of Germans struggling to survive during the time between the two world wars, an era named later by historians as the Weimar Republic.

Ingrid's father, a soldier, who had been conscripted into the German Army in late 1914, was miraculously granted a few days leave to go home before being sent to the notoriously perilous Battle Front in France. He and Hannah had been childhood sweethearts, and when Peter arrived back in Saalfeld the only thing he wanted to do was to marry her. He had loved her ever since he could remember. Their mothers, Eva and Gerta, who were best friends, gave birth to them six weeks apart, and since then they had been inseparable; learning to gurgle to each other as babies, talk and walk as toddlers, and play and squabble as infants.

The wedding ceremony in a local Lutheran Church was small, attended only by their parents and a few close friends. It was a day filled with bitter-sweet feelings. Finally, Peter and Hannah who were just eighteen, declared their undying love for one another in front of the people who mattered most to them, but underlying the joy of that experience was an inescapable feeling of dread; dread that after that day they might never see each other again. If the truth had been known, everyone attending the wedding was going through the same thought process, but the parents, especially the mothers, understood the importance of their commitment to one another in the face of a huge force which could easily tear them apart.

That night, barely a word passed between the young couple; their lovemaking said much more than a thousand words could have done. Sometimes tender, sometimes fierce; their newly-found passion left neither of them in any doubt that they were forever bound to one another. The night was far too precious to waste in oblivion of each other's presence, so when dawn finally came and began to lighten their room they lay peacefully in each other's arms, still wide awake, silently waiting for the day to break.

Within three days of Peters' return to the Front, Hannah knew that she was going to have their child. She was overjoyed. The baby grew quietly in her stomach for ten weeks, and Hanna kept the news to herself. This was something precious between her and Peter and she hugged her growing abdomen every day, feeling a silent connection with him and willing him to be safe.

One March morning as she walked into the kitchen her mother, Eva, gave her a long quizzical look. "Is it my imagination, Hannah, or is my daughter filling out a little around her waist?" The blush which spread upwards from Hannah's neck to her pale cheeks was enough to confirm Eva's suspicions. Holding her daughter's shoulders and kissing her forehead she looked directly into Hanna's eyes, which were brimming with tears. "Don't fret, *liebling*." she said softly, "It won't be long until the war ends. Peter will stay safe and soon, very soon, we will be a real family and all together again."

Within a few days of Eva's suspicions that her daughter was pregnant, a pair of storks came and built their nest on the chimney of the house. It was a little early in the year for that to happen. Storks normally came in late Spring and built their nests all over the region; heralding not only the fact that the sun was finally coming to melt the winter snow, but that there was probably a new baby coming to bless the family living in the house where the nests were laid. If older folk lived in a house where storks nested, it meant that they could expect a long and healthy life, but if a young woman lived there it definitely meant a baby was on the way. It had been the belief that this was so for hundreds of years, and nobody doubted it for one moment; so when the storks came early to Eva and Gustav's house, where Hannah was still living, they gave her great strength and comfort and a feeling of certainty that her baby was divinely blessed.

It is well documented how horrendous life was for the soldiers in the trenches in France; but not only the people serving their militaries suffered. By March 1916, when Hannah was six months pregnant, many inhabitants of Germany were on the brink of starvation. By then, single battles were claiming hundreds of thousands of lives on both sides, and millions of men between the ages of eighteen and fifty five, including Hannah and Peter's fathers, were being sent to the Front to serve in the military.

Both sides in the war had decided that the only way to win it was by targeting the civilian populations, and they proposed to do that by starving them. The German Navy, with their submarines, tried to cut off England's supplies by sabotaging ships full of goods bound for the British Isles, while the British Navy formed a blockade with their ships, and closed off the passages to the North Sea, which virtually prevented all supplies from reaching the German people and their allies.

The tactics worked particularly well for the British. In an impressively short time the lack of goods proved to be a disaster for Europe, but for the German population it was catastrophic. Not only was there a dire lack of food, but actual famine and disease began to sweep across the country.

With virtually all able-bodied men fighting at the Front, women and children all over Europe had to step into their men's shoes and take over jobs in agriculture and industry. In England and France, the Governments were helping to supply essential commodities and food to their populations which made day to day living much easier, but in Germany the people had to fend for themselves.

Food was much harder to come by in the towns and urban areas where the people suffered most. While women worked, they sent their children into the countryside to forage for anything they could find to bring a little comfort; a few potatoes, wheat spelt, a log to burn or a couple of lumps of coal.

With the absence of their husbands Eva and Gerta were forced to find work, which was scarce to non-existent in the area. With most business owners at the Front, the only employment available across the country was in one way or another connected to the war effort, and not much of that was in the region. Although the area was rich in minerals and had once supported many working mines, the Government was focused on getting armed, so only the mines containing iron ore were at that time operational.

Many women, including Eva, Gerta and Hannah, tried to get work in the agricultural areas, which were a long way from Saalfeld in less mountainous land, but without men to do the heavy work most farms had been reduced to producing pitifully small amounts of produce and needed no extra help. After weeks of lining up all day long outside food stores in the town, in the hopes of being able to afford a small bag of flour or some eggs; and with inflationary prices finally making it impossible to buy anything at all, even if the goods were miraculously available, Gerta and Eva finally applied, and were given jobs, at an iron foundry four miles outside Saalfeld, where once only men had been employed. Iron bolts and components were forged there for the German shipyards, and the foundry supervisors were under enormous pressure from the Government and Navy to keep the supplies coming, so the employees had to work from early morning until late at night with no breaks.

It was tough, dirty work and the two friends were only able to obtain the jobs because most women could not handle the heat of the furnaces and the weight of the iron bars. They had both worked in family businesses since they were young girls: Eva in her Father's bakery where she became used to the heat of the ovens and carrying heavy sacks of flour; and Gerta in her Uncle's Mill, where hauling heavy bags of grain was a daily necessity. The rigors of both activities had helped to strengthen their limbs and stamina somewhat, but at that time in history people aged far more quickly than they do now, and at forty three years old both women were well into their middle age and not as tough as they used to be. On top of the grueling work, the walk to the foundry in the early hours of the morning and back late at night was onerous. Earthquakes in the Fourteenth Century had created hills and mountains throughout the entire region, so part of the journey each day was more of a climb than a walk.

Even though youth was on her side, the work was much too hard for Hannah in her condition, but she desperately wanted to help her own and Peter's mother, so each day she left home with them in the early morning hours. The journey was difficult as they had to walk in darkness along narrow, winding, hilly roads. They passed through tiny villages whose inhabitants still lay sleeping, and tried to avoid falling over rocks and boulders and up-rooted trees, which occasionally came crashing down the mountainsides and landed on the road. Once they arrived at the foundry, Hannah would continue walking on into an area of small farming communities, where she spent the day searching for things to eat and to burn.

Finding food was unbelievably hard. It was early spring, but in that part of the world nothing began to sprout and grow until the sun had been out for several weeks and warmed the earth. Mostly, she spent the entire day with her head bent, her eyes focused on the ground, in an effort to spot anything which might be edible. If she raised her eyes for only a moment she might miss something and that could not be permitted to happen. As she scavenged the fields and hedgerows Hannah began to long for the summer, when berries would be growing in the hedgerows and trees loaded with hazel nuts would provide easy harvesting and much-needed nourishment.

Once, after searching about all day and finding nothing around the edges of some fields which had been harvested the year before, Hannah began to feel a sense of growing anxiety. Her back ached from being bent over for hours at a time and her neck and shoulders were stiff and painful, but she was determined to keep searching. She was concerned that Eva and Hannah would be hungry after another grueling day at the foundry and she just couldn't let them down; neither could she starve her baby who depended so much on her for nourishment. The thought of her child made her re-double her efforts to find something, but in the gathering dusk it became more and more difficult to see anything and the desperation she began to feel brought a flood of tears to her eyes, which fell in droplets to the unyielding soil below. She raised her head to brush the tears off her cheeks and rub her eyes with the back of her hand, and through her misty vision she saw in the far distance something large and round in the center of the farm track.

The thing appeared to be moving; but quite often since being pregnant, especially after keeping her head in a bent position and her eyes focused on the ground, she would feel quite giddy when she looked up. As she walked towards the object in the dwindling light, the movement stopped and she was able to observe some detail on it. The outside edge appeared to be curly and it was undoubtedly a pale shade of green. Hannah's heart began to beat a little faster. It couldn't be what she was beginning to think it was; that would be a small miracle. Or could it be?

She began to run; breathlessly jumping and hopping over grooves in the track left by the wheels of heavy carts, and within a few seconds there was no doubt left in her mind. Lying on the ground was a large, slightly battered cabbage! Laughing and crying at the same time she bent down to pick it up. It was heavy, at least two kilos, and apart from a small area where some leaves had been scuffed off – presumably when it fell to the ground off the back of a cart – it was a perfect specimen of its kind. Hannah took off the apron she was wearing, and placing the cabbage in the center she carefully wrapped it up and then tied the long strings of the apron back around her waist, making sure that the weight of the hefty vegetable rested on her hip.

That night there was wonderful cabbage soup for the three hungry women, prepared joyfully over a log fire by a delighted Hannah, after arriving home an hour before her two mothers.

Although everyone in the town suffered from hunger, at the start of the British blockade when the results of the deprivation to come had not yet resonated throughout the country, people were more willing to share what they had in their larders with friends and neighbors. In a country boasting millions of acres of rich farmland and superior dairy herds, it was hard for people to imagine that they could ever be hungry; but very quickly, with half of the able-bodied population fighting and dying in France, the ones left behind began to jealously guard their spoils: especially if it had taken a whole days walking and foraging around to find it.

Hannah continued walking into the countryside, but with each passing day she noticed more and more people were doing the same thing as she was, which made finding anything edible even more difficult. Some of the food seekers were very young children, sent by their mothers to find whatever they could to help keep the family alive. Some came with older siblings, but occasionally children as young as five or six could be seen alone, and it broke Hannah's heart, especially as deep down inside she knew that these searches were all about self-preservation and the survival of the fittest. If she found a couple of potatoes or a turnip she would keep them and take them home for herself and her own family.

Hannah was already painfully thin. For the past few weeks the baby in her belly had not appeared to grow at all, and although she had said nothing to her mother, Hannah was afraid that her lack of nourishment was the cause. It was clear to her that Eva was anxious about the baby, for on several occasions she had tried to make Hannah eat some of her own meager rations, which Hannah had vehemently refused. Eva was exhausted from working in the foundry and she looked every night as though she could faint from fatigue. There was no way that Hannah would deprive her mother of even a mouthful; but even so, she worried about the child she carried, and she prayed every night to God and St. Peter, who her husband had been named after, that they would watch over her and her unborn infant.

Four hundred years previously, a Benedictine Abbey named the Abbey of Saint Peter had existed in Saalfeld. It was destroyed in 1525 during a peasant uprising and another Church had been built on the site, but Saint Peter's name had survived and been magnified through the Ages to the extent that nobody who prayed to him believed he would let them down. As the three women walked to the foundry each morning they kept each other's spirits up by talking about anything positive they could think of. The nesting storks were referred to constantly; the presence of storks at the home of Eva and Gustav absolutely indicated that a baby was coming, and when the female bird settled down on her eggs and waited for them to hatch it was a day of special significance for them all. The majority of the people in Saalfeld were Catholic, and they were also highly superstitious. Many high hopes were hinged on tenuous and irrational belief systems, especially when the name of a Saint was invoked; so while Eva, Gerta and Hannah silently grieved the absence of their husbands, they basically put their safe return into the hands of Saint Peter, while they struggled in a daily battle to survive themselves.

One morning, Hannah was clambering up a hillside when a rabbit ran across her path. 'If only I could catch it,' she thought, 'what a treat; and no worries about food for several days.' The rabbit ran upwards towards the top of the hill and then disappeared into a burrow. Hannah decided to quietly approach the burrow from behind and sit and wait for it to re-emerge with a heavy tree branch in her hand. The weapon was not hard to find, since small trees were dotted all over the area, so once armed, Hannah crept quietly back to the vicinity of the burrow and made her approach.

Her mouth watered as she sat waiting for the head of the rabbit to appear. She imagined the feast she would prepare that night for herself and her two mothers. She would pick wild garlic on the way home and stew it in a pot with the rabbit over the fire. She had gathered plenty of logs the day before, so the fire would burn long enough to cook the meat. She waited patiently for several hours on the hillside, her hand clutching the tree limb and her eyes never wavering from the rabbit hole; but as the day wore on she began to feel tired. She started day-dreaming about her little baby, whom she was convinced was a boy; how she would play with him, and love him, and keep him safe until his daddy came home. And as she dreamed, her eyelids began to feel heavy and her head started to droop.

Suddenly, under her almost closed lids, Hannah caught a glimpse of movement! The rabbit's head appeared out of his hole and he began sniffing the air. Hannah's hand gripped the branch while she raised her arm and made ready to strike; but the rabbit either caught her scent or heard the limb come swooping down toward him, and he let out a strange little yelp and bolted away down the hill. Hannah reached forward as he went, but as she stretched out and lifted her arm to have one more try at hitting him, she tried struggling to her feet at the same time and lost her balance. Down she went; rolling and tumbling down the hill. Over, and over, and over …

By the time she reached home it was very late. She had lain at the foot of the hill for quite some time until searing cramps jerked her awake, and then she sat in the grass with her arms wrapped around her knees, rocking back and forth in an agony of dread and fear, fear and dread, until the pain subsided and concern over Gerta and Eva's alarm for her whereabouts made her move. She was usually home an hour or two before them, and she knew that however much discomfort she was in, she had to get home. When she was halfway there, the cramps kicked in again, and this time they were not going away.

This time, she didn't even need to pray to Saint Peter – he knew about her plight. A farmer shortly came by in a horse-drawn cart, and Hannah waved him to stop. When she explained what had happened he carefully helped her on to the cart and kindly offered to take her all the way home. He made her as comfortable as he could in the back of the cart so that he could keep an eye on her, laying her down on a bed of straw and covering her with some hop sacks to help keep her from shivering; but as a man who had dealt with mother nature and her vagaries all his life, he was deeply concerned about the young woman in his care.

It was a very bumpy ride home. The farmer did his best to keep his horse steady and the wheels in the same worn grooves on the dirt road, but even the slightest jolt produced a shock of pain and a pitiful cry from Hannah. When they reached her house, he walked her to the door and asked if there was anything more he could do to help – but by then there was nothing.

Eva had opened the door for her daughter with a feeling of immense relief which turned instantly to concern when she saw Hannah's condition which was near collapse. Clutching the blood-soaked sacking to her shaking body, Hannah took one look at her mother and wailed.

It was a terrible night. Eva and Gerta eventually persuaded Hannah to give them her tiny dead baby, a little boy. They all repeated a prayer over him and, still wrapped in the sacking, they buried him in the small garden at the back of the house.

Chapter Twelve

By the time the war ended in 1918, the poverty of the people in Germany was staggering. The entire population was on the brink of starvation, existing largely on turnips. Hope was a feeling that most people had given up having, years before.

Saalfeld had residents who had once been considered to be amongst the elite: descendants of noblemen whose ancestors had occupied the area for centuries; mine owners who had employed many people to dig for semi-precious stones and minerals, ochre, iron and slate, all of which abounded in the area; past owners of breweries and brick manufacturers. The list of prosperous people in Saalfeld was long, but soon money meant nothing; differences of class between rich and poor had been obliterated. The only social distinctions which existed depended upon whether a person had something to eat or not.

In a battle which came to be known as 'The Blackest Day of the German Army', the Battle of Amiens, where the Germans were outnumbered six to one by the attacking troops, both Hannah's father and father-in-law had been killed. They were amongst an estimated 30,000 German troops who perished in that conflict and the sad part of it was that they had managed to survive until the war was almost at an end.

Hannah had no news of Peter, and had almost given up hope that she would ever see him again when, one day while she was sitting at the spinning wheel in her parents' kitchen, the door opened and in limped her husband. It was an entirely different Peter who stood in front of her and looked at her with glazed, unseeing eyes.

Eventually, when his body had healed as much as it was going to, he managed to find a job in a local iron mine, but the work was unreliable and dangerous and after being employed there for a very short time, the mine closed. Germany had been banned from making armaments since losing the war, and the once thriving industry of mining iron ore in the area, subsequently deteriorated into such bad shape that the majority of mines became dysfunctional, and either limped along with skeleton staffs or had to close.

In the late 1930's Germany began to re-arm itself and the mines started to flourish again, but for many years mining, along with countless other industries, floundered and fell. At that time the whole of Europe and North America was besieged with economic distress as a result of the fall of the American Stock Market which had repercussions that echoed around the world. That period was named The Great Depression and it lasted in the memories of millions for generations to come.

Peter begged for a job in a local iron foundry, but as the sources of iron were drying up on a daily basis employees were just not needed; so he was turned away. For several months, being turned away was the only constant in both Peter and Hannah's lives. Just to put a little bread on the table they were willing to work in any capacity, but there was simply no work to be had. The whole country was staggering under massive inflation and it was only getting worse.

The people of Germany were, arguably, in a graver situation than many others; since their Government owed so much money in reparations to countries they had damaged during the war, nothing was left to invest in their own infrastructure. Up until the Stock Market crash, financial loans from America had enabled the German Reich to pay their debts, but afterwards, no more money was forthcoming; so Germany found itself on the brink of disaster. By 1935, the country, literally, had no money left.

The entire area around Saalfeld, where Peter and Hannah lived, was rich in stone, slate and minerals and had formerly been a flourishing, successful community; but one by one the mines had closed, and the impact upon the entire community was disastrous.

One day in 1930, when Germany was, certainly, at its lowest economic point, Hannah realized without a doubt that she was pregnant.

She was almost thirty five years old and having a child was something she and Peter had given up hoping for many years before. To begin with, they couldn't afford to feed another hungry mouth, and they also felt that their country was in such bad shape that any child they might have would face a wretched future indeed.

Bleak prospects or not however, the fat was already in the fire, and deep down inside their hearts they must have felt that a new life always brought new hope; so Peter and Hannah decided to give this unexpected event in their lives a fighting chance. After much agonizing and discussion they put what few possessions they owned into a push-cart, and began walking in a North-Easterly direction, toward the agricultural farmlands of West Prussia.

Farms were also suffering at that time. Crop prices had fallen by forty to sixty percent and farmers and their families could barely survive themselves, let alone anyone they tried to hire.

They were both dangerously undernourished, and Hannah was convinced that by the time they walked to the next village her baby would be in great jeopardy. But the hardy little fetus hung in with all its might, and when Ingrid was born and had her first glimpse of the world, she was a sickly, scrawny little thing indeed.

The weeks turned into months and the months turned into years, and the routine at *Munster Walde* remained the same. The girls had now become, on the surface anyway, thoroughly indoctrinated into the rules and regulations of the Third Reich. Their "schooling" was scant indeed when it came to academics like science, history and mathematics, but in the projected ways of the future Reich they were abundantly clear.

CHAPTER THIRTEEN

Ingrid and Ruth became fast friends, albeit well below the radar of their supervisors. The fearless, tall Ruth, and the opinionated tiny Ingrid were a force indeed amongst a crowd of mostly frightened and misguided young women. Helga was the only other girl who Ruth and Ingrid totally trusted, since she and Ruth had embarked two years previously on this adventure to hell together, and they had known one-another their entire lives.

Whenever they had a chance to talk unobserved Ruth and Ingrid discussed plans to escape from their captors, and Helga, the quietly thoughtful voice of reason, became the de-facto referee. Once a vague notion was formed between Ruth and Ingrid, they included Helga in the plan. If Helga had a bad feeling about their idea they would scrap it entirely and try to cook up an alternative. The supervision surrounding their lives was so intense that these conversations were, if truth be told, partly daydreams. A means to help keep their spirits up in the face of a complete lack of knowledge about the outside world. They knew that unless all three of them were completely confident in their plan it just wouldn't work, and then they would find themselves in an even more miserable situation with severe punishment being meted out. They were under no illusions.

Two girls in the school, to their knowledge, had at different times "disappeared" after receiving stringent punishments for relatively minor offenses. One girl had refused to take the medications they were forced to ingest every month. The pills made her react very badly and when it was discovered she was spitting them out she was sent to stand in the quadrangle outside for 48 hours with no food and in below zero temperatures. The poor little thing froze to death and was rapidly wrapped up in sacking and pushed away in a handcart; no doubt to be hidden away in one of the many stables, then buried when the ground was no longer frozen. Nobody knew what had happened to the second girl. The circumstances under which she disappeared were shrouded in secrecy throughout the entire school, and nobody dared to ask about her. It was as though a directive had been issued, albeit silently, that the same thing could happen to anyone who had the temerity to enquire as to her whereabouts. So nobody did.

When Ingrid and Ruth had almost run out of ideas to escape, the best one of all fell right into their laps! It simply needed a huge amount of conviction and courage to execute it. They were in music class one day when Fraulein Schmidt introduced a newcomer. A short balding man of wide girth and ruddy complexion, with a huge handlebar mustache, small feet and pudgy fingers. Ruth thought he looked a lot like her perception of Humpty Dumpty and had a hard time suppressing a giggle, while Fraulein Schmidt explained to the class that this was Herr Manfred Tolle. He was from the city of Kaunas in Lithuania, which was at that time occupied by the Germans, where he was a conductor at the Musical Academy of Kaunas.

Herr Tolle, Freulein Schmidt explained, was there to hear each member of the class perform individually. Once he had formed an opinion he was going to select three class members to perform in a music festival near Kaunas. The festival was one week hence, so the selected students would have time to practice intensely every day until absolutely perfect; which was a very important achievement, since the winning students at the festival would enable the judges to bestow preferential favors to their individual schools.

When the details had been explained to the students, Ruth, Ingrid and Helga exchanged glances, and between the three, in those innocent expressions, a thousand unspoken words were communicated.

Each student was summarily instructed to stand in front of the class and perform to the best of their ability. Some were instrumentalists and played their favorite pieces on their violins, flutes, accordions or piano. Others sang a few verses of their chosen songs; mostly German ones, but occasionally a student sang a classical piece which was also acceptable.

Fraulein Schmidt played the piano accompaniment for the students who sang, while Herr Tolle, a baton clutched between his pudgy fingers, conducted the girls, nodding his head in time to the beat and pacing around in half-circles on his tiny feet.

As the morning progressed and each girl performed, the expression on Herr Tolle's face barely changed. In fact, one could deduce an almost resigned, even bored look in his eyes. Several of the students performed very well, but it soon became clear that Herr Tolle was looking for excellence and nothing less. When it was Ingrid's turn to sing, she felt a frisson of fear run through her body. Would she be good enough? But the knowledge that this test was presenting her with an opportunity to escape back to the loving arms of her parents, gave her the courage to do her very best. Standing next to the piano at the front of the class, she nodded toward Frau Schmidt and told her what she was going to sing. Taking a deep breath, she pulled her little frame up to its highest point, raised her chin and placed her palms together. Frau Schmidt struck the first note, and the voice of an angel rose to the cracked plaster ceiling of the schoolroom.

Its' sweetness and clarity was so pure and innocent that for a moment Herr Tolle looked sharply across at Ingrid in surprise, while dropping his baton in the process. The class watched it clatter across the floor, while Herr Tolle, with great difficulty, bent his portly body down to retrieve it. Meanwhile, Fraulein Schmidt continued playing the piano while Ingrid sang valiantly on, each note sounding sweeter and stronger than the last. When her aria came to an end the entire class fell absolutely silent. There was a short period when it felt as though the girls wanted to applaud their classmate, but rules were so strict they were reluctant to show their support. An awkward moment arose, but suddenly, quite naturally, Herr Tolle himself tucked his recovered baton under his arm and brought his pudgy hands together in an enthusiastic spasm of applause. Ingrid bowed quickly to the class, then quickly to Herr Tolle, and scuttled back to her seat with an expression of frozen modesty, even shock.

The next few girls' performances brought back the look of resignation to Herr Tolle; and then it was Helga's turn. Helga's voice was deep and rich, almost baritone, and the only one amongst all the girls with such a sound. Since there were no boys in the school, Helga's voice was in constant demand, and perhaps since she sang so much she had honed her voice with all the practice into an especially valuable instrument. Herr Tolle seemed extremely impressed when Helga's song was over. He didn't applaud her, but he beamed at her and Fraulein Schmidt and nodded his head with such enthusiasm that it was clear he was beginning to feel his visit to Munster Walde had not been in vain.

Ruth was the last one to perform. She was already the acknowledged most talented in the class, which was why, she supposed, Fraulein Schmidt had held her back to the end. She walked to the piano and asked Fraulein Schmidt to please allow her to accompany herself. Herr Tolle's attention was immediately peaked. His bushy eyebrows raised in surprise as Fraulein Schmidt pushed back on her stool and allowed Ruth to take her seat in front of the piano. Ruth paused for a few seconds before lifting her hands over the keys. She was banking everything on this performance! It was the perfect chance to escape from Munster Walde if she was selected to represent the school. She knew that not only her musical talent would be weighed, but also her patriotism. An index finger struck the first note and there was no going back. Ruth's rendition of Deutschland Uber Alles was befitting of a mature opera singer. The strength and clarity in her voice was a joy to hear, and the power and confidence in her piano playing belied her 15 years.

When the final note was played and the last chord had soared to the heavens, Ruth stood and bowed first to her teacher and then to Herr Tolle. The entire class applauded, not seeming to care at all about the consequences, and Ruth quietly returned to her desk. Herr Tolle's face had turned a strange shade of purple. One could have misconstrued the change in color as a cause for alarm, but under the present circumstances it was clear that the rotund man was thoroughly excited.

Herr Tolle waddled across the classroom as fast as his small feet and short legs would allow, and sat down on the piano stool which Ruth had vacated. Fraulein Schmidt was closing the lid on the instrument and she turned to face him as he sat. "Well, Herr Tolle," she said, "what did you make of our students' performances?" "Fraulein Schmidt," Herr Tolle replied, mopping his brow, "I'm most impressed, most impressed. I can report to you now, and I'm delighted to tell you that I have selected three of your students to represent Munster Walde at the Grande Festival".

Left unsaid by the teacher and the musical conductor was the true reason for the 'Festival' which was actually a Music Camp. Talented children were being sent to the Camp to help raise the morale of the German soldiers. Russian troops had already been seen a few kilometers from the border, and German soldiers were getting prepared to be pushed back. The German officers were finding it harder to keep their men's attitudes positive, so the Performance was being held to show the men how well this selected group of German youth were responding to their training. The theory being that if the children were strong and optimistic in their Leaders, then surely grown men would be too.

Ruth, Ingrid and Helga were, to nobody's surprise, selected to represent Munster Walde. That night they could barely eat supper, they were so nervous and excited. No words passed between them until lights out when they breathlessly huddled together between their bunk beds and whispered their thoughts. Ingrid thought they should not even enter the contest; just jump off the train on the way there and head for the woods where they could hide out and eventually make their way home. Helga and Ruth both felt they should go to Kaunas and sing at the Camp; then on the way back to school they should make their escape. Their reasoning made sense. If they were registered as having entered the contest they would raise less suspicion and the supervisors in both locations would trust them to return to their school – especially if they performed well at the Camp. If they escaped on the return journey the alarm might not be raised until the train arrived in Munster Walde, by which time they could be well on the way to their homes.

This somewhat loose plan was agreed upon, and for the next week the girls practiced all day every day. They were completely unaware that danger in the form of Russian Troops was closing in, and that every man in the area capable of standing and breathing was being recruited to bolster up the declining numbers of German soldiers. She did not know it, but Ruth's father, who was in his mid-fifties was drafted to join the Army, along with his older brother, both of whom were actually not considered fit enough to fight for their country; but by this time the German authorities were desperate to save their last considered stronghold in Europe, so any able man, just capable of bearing a weapon, young or old, weak or strong, was forced into the military.

The girls, of course, were oblivious to these events, which in essence meant that while German civilians would normally have been keeping a watchful eye on the activities in their region, there were now far less watchful eyes!

As the time to leave for the Music Camp drew ever closer, the three girls were given new dirndls to wear at the event. Little booklets with rules and regulations were handed to them on the morning of their departure, with instructions on their behavior on the train and when they arrived at the Camp; what they should say and what they should do.

They all took the little bags of belongings they had brought when they first came to Munster Walde, containing nightwear, their new dirndls, a few grooming essentials and, from the kitchen, a small package containing a thick slice of heavy grain bread, a chunk of cheese and a green apple from the fruit trees in the garden of Munster Walde.

Frederick Brehm brought the horse and cart around to the front door of the house, and the three girls climbed in. A huge muddle of nervousness and excitement jostled about in their hearts and minds, but the overriding feeling was that of anticipation. Perhaps, finally, their dearest wish to be reunited with their families could be realized. A few of the older students came to give them brief 'good luck and good journey' wishes and hurried back to their chores before being noticed missing, and as the old horse clip-clopped slowly out of the courtyard, the girls were already imagining they would never see Munster Walde again.

1. Ruth in America

2. Ruth 1941

3. Ruth age 13. Just before going to the children's Camp

4. Ruth age 17

5. Ruth 1947 After leaving the camp in Denmark

6. Agusta with baby Barbara

7. Ruth with Barbara

8.Ruth in Freudenstadt

9. Ruth in Freudenstadt celebrating Fasching. The first time she sang in public since the concert at the second camp

10. Ruth and Barbara in 1956

11. Ruth with her parents and Magrid

12. Ruth with Barbara before leaving for Amerika

13. Ruth with her friend Charles and the author

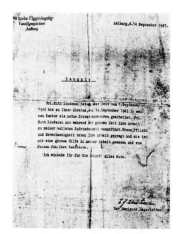

14. The letter written by Commander Anderson, in hopes of ensuring Ruth's safe passage to Germany

IN MEMORY

Ruth Charlotte Raible

October 18, 1929 - September 4, 2017

11. Ruth in Memoriam

CHAPTER FOURTEEN

Once on the train and truly on their way to the Music Camp, the three young girls finally breathed a huge sigh of relief. The competition ahead was the last thing on their minds, although every waking hour of the previous week had been taken up practicing for their performance.

"When we are in the dormitory we must try to find some blankets to take for our escape," said Ruth. "It will be very cold at night, and we will need something to stay warm." "What about food?" said Ingrid, "We will need to take food. There might be some good food at the Hostel where we stay, so we should be taking extra. Especially food like boiled eggs, bread, cheese and apples which can keep for a few days".

The return train to Munster Walde only ran once a day, so the girls would be staying two nights in Kaunas and returning on the third day. On the second day, the day of their performance, the train would have already left, so this gave the girls a greater opportunity to find the supplies they would need, to prepare for their daring escape.

The minute they alighted from the train in Kaunas they were surprised to be immediately approached, almost pounced upon, by a uniformed officer of the German Army. He appeared to be in his mid-thirties, with a slim build, a pock-marked face and an expression more like a grimace than a smile of welcome. His arrival was so abrupt and unexpected that the girls were quite taken by surprise. Stepping, it seemed, automatically up to Ruth as the tallest of the three, indeed he was only an inch or two taller than she. He clicked his heels together and thrust his neck forward, stopping about four inches in front of her face. "Fraulein Lindenau?" He barked out his enquiry, and Ruth raised her green eyes to meet his in wide amazement. Her look must have melted a tiny corner of his heart as his expression softened when she shyly answered. "Yes, Mein Herr, I am she, and this is Fraulein Wenzel and Fraulein Vogel. We are here to sing at the Camp". "Well, very good," the officer replied, visibly impressed with the attractive young woman's manner, "I am Captain Carl Hoelzel, assisting Herr Tolle with the Musical Camp, and I'm here to escort you to the dormitories." "Many thanks, Herr Captain," Ruth replied, her expression of astonishment replaced by one of relief. "That is most kind of you." The Captain's smile spoke volumes. He had clearly been expecting to meet three children and was pleasantly surprised to find they were all young women. Ruth and Helga were both very attractive and tall for their ages and although Ingrid was petite, she was also a young beauty with a confident, adult bearing, so the three young women, in the eyes of Captain Hoelzel, were a pleasure to behold.

Reaching for Ruth's leather traveling bag, he clutched the handles with his left hand and swung the bag over his shoulder before grabbing the bags of Ingrid and Helga – holding them both in his right hand. Then looking Ruth directly in the eyes, he said "Follow me Frauleins." Shy Ruth was completely used to doing as she was told, along with all the other girls at Munster Walde, but something imperceptible was tapping at her sub-conscious, the same feeling that tapped when she had spoken to the young soldier several weeks earlier, when she had asked him about the situation with the war. It was a feeling that the young men were somehow attracted to her – but it was only with the eye contact and she couldn't be certain. It was just the dawning of a new idea, which gave her a small, fluttery feeling in her stomach.

The captain took the girls to a battered-looking military vehicle parked outside the railway station, and he swung the bags into the open rear end. Then, opening a passenger door he guided Ingrid and Helga into the back seat, and Ruth into a front seat next to himself. The journey was not far. It lasted about half an hour, but all the way to their destination the girls saw broken-down German vehicles, burned-out houses and piles of rubble at the side of the road. By the time they reached the "Music Camp" Ruth was bursting with questions. "Herr

Captain, what has happened here? This isn't a city. It looks like this area is destroyed. Are we really supposed to be singing in this place?" "You are here to sing," was the curt reply, "and I can assure you this is the correct place."

The captain swung the vehicle into a rapid left turn and stopped at a gate wrapped in barbed wire, which was opened by a uniformed soldier. It was only then that the girls realized they were approaching a makeshift military barracks. Soldiers were scurrying everywhere and rather than looking like a spic and span encampment, it looked more like a place where people were making a hasty retreat. Some large vehicles were parked in line, loaded with bursting khaki bags and what looked like sacks of flour and provisions, and in the distance a horn was impatiently hooting out signals which could be heard all over the campground, causing various reactions of movement and speed. In front of a brick building, seemingly in the center of all this chaos, was where Captain Hoelzel brought the vehicle to a resounding, skidding stop; stirring up clouds of dust and gravel as he did so. He leapt out, telling the girls to stay where they were until he returned.

As soon as they were alone, the girls looked at one another in complete dismay. "Where is this place?" "What is going on here?" "Surely we can't be singing here. This is a place for soldiers, not for music and singing". "And where is Herr Tolle? Shouldn't he be here to meet us?" They were baffled beyond belief and not a little frightened. As was often the way, the girls looked to Ruth for answers, and as she always did, she stepped up to the task, albeit with a completely unknown set of circumstances before her.

"It looks," she said, "as though the enemy is approaching and that everyone here is ready to retreat. I think we must get away like everyone else, but we will stick to our plan and try to escape separately. I will ask Herr Captain Hoelzel exactly what the situation is. I will tell him we want to go back to Munster Walde and perhaps he will escort us back to the train station. When we are there, we will try to make our escape".

The girls nodded in assent. They were in truth blindly following Ruth's suggestions as, for the first time in three years, they were experiencing life without rules and boundaries. With all the chaos around them, it felt as though Ruth was now their rock. The person to whom they owed allegiance. Even as they sat in the battered Army truck, ever more chaos surrounded them. Vehicles were careening about everywhere – trying to exit buildings and the encampment. Where the Music Camp was situated was never discovered, though a large group of boys and girls holding musical instruments were observed by Ruth as they were ushered into a vehicle by a group of bewildered-looking soldiers.

The chaos around them continued; some groups of soldiers behaving in an almost frenzied state of panic. Shouting and careering about the garrison in such disarray, it was as though regimentation and discipline had been suspended and thrown to the winds! After what seemed like an age of waiting, Captain Hoelzel, looking quite red-faced and decidedly more flustered than his previous calm exterior, came running back to the truck carrying a military back-pack and a battered canvas hold-all. He threw both items into the back of the truck on top of the girls' bags and jumped into the driver's seat, while simultaneously switching on the engine and turning the steering wheel into a position ready for take-off!

The girls had seen it all by now, and hardly needed to ask. As the wheels of the truck squealed and screeched on the tarmac while doing an almost 365 degree turn, it was clear that the entire barracks was in retreat and that the Music Camp was a vision which would never be realized. Captain Hoelzel waited until they were through the barbed-wire gate and driving on the road back to the Railway Station in Kaunas, before he said anything. "Fräuleins, I am obliged to tell you that a special train has been ordered, a train which is going to Germany. Herr Tolle left yesterday evening with twenty students who were here to perform. He left instructions that all remaining students be taken care of today, and sent back to their respective schools. The Russian Army is reputedly approaching and the entire Camp is retreating. My instructions are to escort you back to Munster Walde, where you will be met at the Bartenstein Bahnhof and taken back to your school."

All three girls were dying inside. Their carefully laid plans were, in an instant, crushed. Any communication they had with one another was purely facial, as they had learned in Munster Walde. Eyes opened wide in dismay; lips pursed together; one countenance after another expressed their feelings to one another without saying a single word. The un-uttered accepted circumstance was that they must now comply to the Captain's orders.

Once at the Railway Station, the Captain took all three girls in tow, and entered a little office inside the entrance where a tired-looking, elderly man wearing a Station Master's uniform sat on a high-legged stool, his elbow leaning heavily on a small shelf. "Yes, Herr Captain!" His body sprung into a semblance of an upright position, and he scrambled to his feet. "What can I do for you, Herr Captain?" "My vehicle is parked outside, Mein Herr," answered Captain Hoelzel. Someone from the Camp will be here to collect it within the next twenty-four hours. Please make certain it is secure." "Yes, of course Herr Captain. It will be done, rest assured." The Captain bowed his head, clicked his heels, and told the girls to go to the platform with him. The wait was very long. The train had been ordered specifically to gather up military personnel along the route, so the going was very slow. Traditionally, German trains were never late, but in times of War everything was turned upside-down. After several hours, when evening was over and night had fallen, the much awaited train chugged it's way in to the station.

Tumbling into their seats, the girls were already tired, but they had determined to try and stay awake to see what was happening everywhere. The journey was predictably slow. As always, the train stopped at every small hamlet along the way, and try as they might the girls were unable to pry any more information from Captain Hoelzel. Ruth asked him one question after another and his answer was always the same, "I am permitted to say nothing. My orders are only that you young ladies are returned to the officials at Munster Walde, that is all."

All along the railway route, the girls looked for signs of information – anything to give them a clue about what was happening in the Region, but mostly the train tracks ran through wooded or agricultural areas which pitch black in the night showing only the shadows of trees and bushes. Only in the small villages where the trains stopped were there signs of a different nature than normal. Far more military personnel than local people were mounting the passenger carriages, and more heavy-looking goods, some of them huge and canvas-wrapped, were being loaded into the rear open carts of the train. Again, a sign that military people were in a hurry to leave the area. The word of advancing Russian Troops had clearly been signaled ahead. The German Army was in retreat.

"Herr Captain, how far away do you think the Red Army is?" Demanded Ruth in a frightened voice. "So many soldiers are getting on the train, but no civilians. Will the people in the villages be left to suffer attacks? Has the German Army warned the civilians as well?" Stating these obvious facts to the Captain, he just stared ahead. He was like a man in a trance. He knew nothing and he said nothing. His ultimate destination was unknown to the girls, but it clearly wasn't Munster Walde. He could have been given orders to join up with his comrades in a far-away place, or been told to report back to Headquarters back in Germany; the bags he brought with him certainly indicated he was going somewhere. They simply didn't know. When they eventually arrived at the Munster Walde Bahnhof he watched them like a hawk. Each girl was escorted individually to the platform with her bag, and when a cart arrived to collect the girls, he took all three bags and walked off the platform to the waiting cart. A relieved look on his face.

Neither of the Brehm brothers was there to meet them at the Bahnhof. The girls were visibly shaken when they alighted from the train and saw Gerde Schmidt barking orders at the Captain to hurry along with the bags and get the girls over to the cart. Ruth knew, as did Ingrid and Helga, that Frau Schmidt carried a weapon at all times. She had been known to threaten many a girl when they were working in the fields; raising the gun in the air she would fire it in pure anger if she spotted a girl stretching her back for a few moments while digging a row of beets or cutting cabbages.

Any ideas that Ruth might have had about making a run for the woods while the Captain's back was turned during the few moments it took to carry their bags to the cart, (and it did cross her mind), were soon dashed! She saw the cruel face of Frau Schmidt quite clearly through the Bahnhof entrance, and she knew without a doubt that had they tried to sprint away each one of them would have been directly in her line of fire.

None of the three girls were the same people as when they had first arrived at Munster Walde. All their senses had been sharpened whether they wanted it or not. The constant, inhuman drilling had also given them a strong sense of survival; a sixth sense, as it were, to know when and where to not put their lives at risk. A hardening of their minds was inevitable in view of the fact that they had been schooled for that very purpose, and each one of them now had as much grit as sentimentality in their characters.

They climbed into the cart, barely acknowledging Frau Schmidt, who simply nodded toward them as they sat on the hard wooden bench. No conversation arose between them as the cart rumbled its' way along the bumpy country roads, Frau Schmidt flicking the old horse's neck with a long whip if she thought it was slowing down.

All three girls nudged each other when they were seated behind Frau Schmidt, and pursed their lips tight in a message to each other to say nothing about their journey. Clearly, Frau Schmidt was in a similar state of obliviousness as to what was exactly happening, and the last thing she would have wanted to do would be to lower herself by asking the three students if they knew what was going on in the Region they had visited. It was a kind of soundless check-mate.

Arriving at the school, the girls sensed an elusive but palpable quietness. It was not yet evening; usually a time when girls could be seen finishing their chores about the gardens. A dog set up a cacophony of barking when he heard their arrival on the courtyard stones, yet neither of the Brehm brothers came running out to fetch the horse for stabling. Instead, Frau Schmidt went into the building and summoned two of the older girls to go outside and un-couple the horse from the cart and put them both in the stables. As the girls hurried towards them, they carried what seemed almost like an air of excitement. Ruth, Ingrid and Helga sensed it, and taking their bags off the cart they stood beside it and waited for the girls to arrive. In a few minutes, Katya Winkler and Lotta Lange came puffing up to them, asking them how the music competition had gone. Both girls were seventeen and had been at Munster Walde since its' inception, two years before Ruth arrived. Their knowledge of the school's workings was well known to them, and they had frequently offered words of advice over the years, which the younger girls had heeded. Ingrid became animated. "There was no Music Camp, no Music

Competition, no Musical Recital! It was all a big lie. When we got to Kaunas it was a Military Base only, outside the city, and all the soldiers there were in retreat! We waited for three hours to be told the Russian Army was near, and that we had to come back here!"

Ingrid wailed the last sentence, and realizing the import of her statement she began to cry. The girls all prodded and nudged her to be quiet. They didn't want anyone , even the other girls seeing this show of emotion. Ruth jumped in and tried to help the situation. "Ingrid," she said, "don't cry, being here is far better than being in Kaunas. In Kaunas we were much further away from our homes. If all the chaos we saw there comes here as well we will have a much better chance to escape." There was a long silence while Ingrid wiped her nose on her sleeve and nodded in assent.

"While you were preparing to go away," said Katya in hushed tones, the Instructors must have got bad news. There was an urgent meeting held here yesterday before you left and within a few hours everything became chaotic. A brother of Fraulein Muller is quite high-ranking in the Army and he warned her that The Russian Army is approaching this entire region. As soon as she knew, she told Frau Schmidt and Fraulein Werner, and the meeting was called."

"How do you know all this?" asked Ruth. "Because," said Katya," little Liesel Bauer had been put on brass-cleaning duties. She was cleaning brass candlesticks in the Instructors Private Sitting Room when the telephone rang. You know it's the only phone in the whole of Munster Walde, and Liesel became nervous when it was ringing so she hid behind a couch. Fraulein Muller was on duty yesterday and she was the one who answered the phone."

"The meeting was called immediately after Fraulein Muller told the news," went on Katya, "and the news of the Russians spread like wildfire." Her voice dropped to a whisper. "This morning, Frederick and Gunther Brehm disappeared from Munster Walde. They have been working here for thirty five years. In the beginning, when it was a fine home for a fine family, and later when it became a military base and then our school. For them to leave now and go back to their family homes it must be a very serious event that is happening."

Ruth, Helga and Ingrid were amazed that in such a short space of time so much had happened, but their recent memories of the fear on soldiers' faces gave them a modicum of courage. "And what is happening here now?" said Ruth. "Do all the girls know what is going on?" "Oh, yes," was the reply, "already forty girls have escaped!"

It was true. Forty unsupervised girls working in the fields had heard the news and they had walked (rather, ran) away from their place of indoctrination. The three supervisors were now in a quandary as to what they should do. 'Headquarters' were no longer sending instructions, as chaos reigned, it seemed, in the entire region. No-one was available to run down the escaping girls, so they just left.

Can anyone imagine the courage this must have instilled in the remaining twenty-five young in-mates? For in-mates they were. "So what is happening with all the other students?" asked Ruth, "Is everyone going to try and escape?" Lotta put her finger to her lips, "After the girls in the fields bolted yesterday we remaining ones are being supervised very carefully. Look!" She indicated a window in the house, where the outline of a figure holding binoculars could be seen. "I don't know which Instructor that is," said Lotta, "but you can be certain she has a gun nearby. Last night we were all made to sleep in one dormitory, and Fraulein Muller slept in a bed right by the door, so we couldn't leave the room."

"What can we do?" wailed Ingrid, I want to go home so badly." "Don't worry, we have another plan to leave but we can't tell you now," said Lotta, we have already been talking far too long. Tomorrow morning at breakfast I will make certain that one of the girls tells you exactly what we have to do."

CHAPTER FIFTEEN

As Helga, Ingrid and Ruth walked towards the back entrance leading to the kitchen, their feelings were a mixture of excitement and dread. Their steps were not hurried and they eyed each other with some trepidation. What to expect when they were inside the building would seem to be anybody's guess! They opened the back door, which led to the back staircase and kitchen, but as they walked down the hallway towards the stairs they were amazed to see that twenty or so heavy sacks of flour were blocking the stairs, and threaded over and above the sacks were strands of barbed wire! "Mein Gott!" burst out of Ruth's mouth, "This looks like a war zone! Let's just go straight to the main staircase and take our bags that way. We will find out soon enough what has happened here."

The usual light buzz of human activity was not apparent when they walked into the main lobby. Under all circumstances no-one was ever allowed to laugh and talk loudly, but on this morning the normal sounds of an early morning household were missing. Noises like the small clatters of china and cutlery being washed in the kitchen after breakfast; the opening and closing of doors as students went to class, or began to attend to their cleaning duties of polishing and dusting, feet walking across the parquet flooring in the main hall. All was suspiciously quiet.

They were just mounting the first few stairs leading up to the dormitories when a loud "Hey, you three!" stopped them in their tracks. Turning around, they saw Fraulein Werner pacing toward them from the Dining Room. "Where do you think you are going?" she yelled, "you should be using the back staircase!" "Sorry, Fraulein," said Helga, we just returned from the Music Camp and we are taking our bags up to our dormitory." "The back staircase was blocked, Fraulein," said Ruth defensively. "We tried to go that way but there were several sacks of flour and wire blocking the stairs."

Fraulein Werner was unaware that the Brehm Brothers had been ordered by Gerde Schmidt to block the staircase the night before, to prevent any more of the girls from escaping during the night. As she slowly absorbed this new information, Fraulein Werner nodded her head. "Yes, I see," she said in a quieter tone, "so you thought you were doing the correct thing by going this way. Well, you have my permission to do so, but your dormitory has now changed. You are no longer in Number Three but in Number Eight on the same floor. All the girls in the school are now sleeping in the same room." "Yes, Fraulein," chorused the girls, and picking their bags up off the stairs they proceeded the climb up to the second floor. "And if you want to have some breakfast," was the parting shot, "get it in the Kitchen!"

The girls were starving having eaten practically nothing for twenty four hours, so even the thought of Munster Walde gruel caused their tummies to rumble. The new Dorm Room was completely full. Twenty six beds crowded every inch of space along the walls, and they had no idea which beds they were assigned to, so they deposited their bags right by the entrance to the room and hurried back down the main staircase. As they made their way to the kitchen, the house was still strangely silent. Magd turned in surprise when she heard them enter. "What are you doing in here, Frauleins?" she said. "Why are you not in the Dining Room?" "Fraulein Muller told us to come here and get some breakfast," said Ingrid. "We just arrived here from a long train ride and we haven't eaten for ages!" "Well, you are very lucky indeed," retorted Magd, giving a little snort, "All the other girls are in the Dining Room being severely punished." "Why?" said all three girls, " What happened? What did they do?" Magd, who could talk a mile a minute when encouraged, pulled up her short, plump frame and adopted an expression of disgust. "As like always," Magd replied, lowering her voice and moving toward them, "they did nothing! They are being punished for what all the other girls did. Yesterday afternoon Forty girls who were working on the fields escaped! They had heard in the morning about Russian troops coming closer, and they made plans together. Frederick Brehm was supposed to be supervising them but the old boy nodded off for a while, just like he often does. The girls knew that, and they were waiting for it to happen, then when he obliged the whole group ran off into the woodlands! Just like that!" She raised her arm and swatted her hand in the air to clarify the point. "So everyone else was punished," stated Ruth, shaking her head. "Yes," Magd went on, "first they all had to move their beds into a single room, then they were told there was no supper. Then, in their nightwear, they had to stand in the courtyard until they almost froze. At midnight Frau Schmidt permitted them to go to bed where they were guarded by Fraulein Muller."

The girls looked at each other in dismay. "And what about this morning?" asked Helga, "It's very quiet in the Dining Room." "All the girls were told to come down at 5:00 AM and stand behind their chairs." said Magd, "For four hours those poor little things have been there - no moving, no speaking and no eating. It's terrible the way these girls are being treated; I can't stand it! I was told not to prepare breakfast today, and I don't know what will happen about lunch. If it wasn't for the fact that I'm able to help a little by giving you all some nourishment, albeit very paltry, I'd run away myself! If you three girls have been given permission to have breakfast I can give you some bread and drippings from the meat I cooked yesterday." "Ohhh! Thank you, Magd, that would be wonderful," said Ruth.

The girls were sitting at the pine table, munching hungrily on their promised hunks of bread and fat drippings, when a loud siren was heard wailing in the distance. It was an alarm signal that enemy troops were no more than a day away. The girls didn't know this, but Magd did. Wardens in the nearby village where she lived had been drilling all the residents to listen out for this sound for the past four years, and Magd knew what it was when she heard it. She dropped what she was doing and ran towards the Dining Room, to warn Fraulein Muller. Ruth, Helga and Ingrid followed. "Fraulein Muller!" "Fraulein Muller!" shouted Magd as she opened the door, "The enemy Army is approaching, we all have to get out!" Her frantic shouting subsided to a murmur as she looked around the room in disbelief. "Ach! Mein Gott! Where is everybody? They've all gone!"

Indeed, the room appeared to be empty. Then Ingrid heard a muffled shuffling noise, seemingly under the dining table. Her eyes opened wide in warning as she put her finger to her mouth and indicated to Ruth and Helga what she suspected. Magd saw her motioning to the table as well, and being a woman entirely lacking a nervous disposition, she immediately dropped to her knees and peered underneath. "Nein! Ach du Lieber Himmel!" No! Good heavens! "Fraulein Muller!" she shrieked. The three girls also got on the floor to peer underneath the table and were astounded to see that indeed it was so! Their bullying Instructor had clearly been on the end of a bullying attack herself, and was now tied up and muffled in a very ungainly position on the floor. The girls were shocked, certainly, but not a little amused. Magd took hold of Fraulein Muller's arm and heaved on it until the woman's body was half out from under the table; by which time the three girls pulled her into a semblance of a sitting position. Magd untied the bandage which was around her head and the girls set to, and began untying the knotted bandages which bound her hands and feet. The woman was clearly still shaken, but it seemed to be more out of anger than shock. "That girl!" she shouted, "Verdammt! Verdammt! Damn! Damn! "She stole bandages from the medical room! That little schlampe, slut, Tilda Huber pretended she twisted her ankle in the fields yesterday and Frau Meyer wrapped bandage around her leg several times, all the way up to her knee. If she had waited an hour longer she could have escaped with all the other girls! I suppose only a few of them had the plan to wait for Herr Brehm to take a nap, stupid Spasti!" Idiot! Magd laid a hand on Fraulein Muller's arm in an attempt to calm her down. "Fraulein Muller, please pay attention to what I am saying," she begged, " the alarm signal has sounded! We have to leave Munster Walde!" Fraulein Muller looked down at the hand on her arm and pulled away as though she had been stung! "Lass mich in ruh!" she yelled, Leave me alone! Still smarting from the fact that a room-full of girls had fooled her, she wasn't in the least bit interested in the urgent news. Pulling herself up into a standing position, the Instructor went on, "Huber didn't even have to smuggle the bandage into the Dining Room this morning, it was brought in right under my nose, wrapped around her damn leg!" Ruth suppressed a smile and thought to herself, 'If these Instructors spend three years making us hard and calculating, lacking all feeling, why are they then surprised if we turn around and play the same game with them? Three years ago we would never have had the courage.'

Fraulein Muller went on, "And they waited until my head was bent when I was eating my breakfast. Then one of them came up behind me and hit me on the head! Look!" she said, pointing to a metal tray on the floor; the tray which had held her breakfast. "That is what they used to hit me!" She touched the top of her head gingerly and winced at the pain, but still she went on. "Then several other girls held me down on the floor and gagged me and tied me up!" "But I brought you your breakfast at 6:00 AM, Fraulein. Do you mean you have been in this predicament since then?" Magd was incredulous. "Yes, these girls were very clever," the Instructor snorted, "I think we have been teaching them too much about courage."

Magd was still anxiously trying to plead with Fraulein Muller when the distant sound of sirens could be heard. The expression on her face froze, and she turned on her heel, blew a kiss at the three girls and ran! Ruth, Helga and Ingrid looked at each other and in their eyes they signaled a message so clear to one another that it could never have been mistaken. 'We are the next to go.'

As it turned out, fate stepped in and helped them more than they could have hoped. Gerde Schmidt, the biggest tyrant of the three Instructors, had been so flabbergasted by the news of the approaching Russian Army that she had locked herself into her little office and waited impatiently for instructions from her Headquarters. Instructions, however, were not forthcoming; lines of communication had been severed. That was the biggest failure she experienced. The people who had indoctrinated her to obey orders at all times had never bothered to imagine that they might be on the losing end, therefore, when things began falling apart she had no idea about how to proceed. Her solution was to hide away in her office and just wait. The tyrant and bully who had cruelly brutalized and intimidated sixty-five young girls was the biggest coward of all.

Fraulein Muller was tempted to wait with Frau Schmidt but eventually took the advice of her brother. She left the school as soon as she could; grabbing a few possessions and packing them into a bag she walked out of the Munster Walde entrance and was never heard of again. Fraulein Werner, always the weaker Instructor, didn't know what she should do. Her dutiful conscience was to the Reich. She was malleable and honest. Everything she did was, she thought, her duty. As the only remaining Instructor in the school, with Fraulein Muller now gone, and Frau Schmidt locked in her office, she was bewildered and confused as to her instructions. She need not have worried too much. Any responsibility she felt she had was soon taken out of her hands. It was ironic that only three girls remained in Munster Walde, Ruth, Helga and Ingrid. Sixty three other girls had scattered themselves all over the countryside, trying to stay free and not captured by the Russians. The stories of what happened to the girls when they were caught were horrific, and recounted many years after the war ended. To say that Russian soldiers were brutal was an understatement. What happened to all those girls was not known by Ruth. She hoped they all managed to escape, but in reality, she only knows her own story.

The alarm sirens sounding off that morning were a day late in warning! Only when the enemy was already in Magd's village, did the Warden sound the alarm, and it was already too late. Men were taken as prisoners out of the fields and houses, and whole areas were being destroyed. The chaos and pandemonium of war had arrived, and it was only a matter of time before it would come knocking on the door at Munster Walde.

Chapter Sixteen

After seeing Magd leave, and then Fraulein Muller, the girls decided to go in search of Fraulein Werner. With all rules and regulations tossed out of the window, as it were, they had no fear of searching all the rooms in the house. They finally found her in the Instructors' Living Room, sitting on a window seat, gazing out onto the courtyard and the main entrance. Anyone coming to the house would have to come this way, so Fraulein Werner had a good position to survey all activities.

When the girls entered the room Fraulein Werner showed no surprise. She turned her head to look at them, then patted the window seat, indicating for them to come and join her. All traces of her abrupt forcefulness had disappeared. "Well, Frauleins," she said quietly, "it looks like we are about to be captured by the enemy." "Nooooo," shrieked Ingrid, "Never! Never! We must hide!"

It was as though Ingrid had pulled a plug and all the water was escaping through a plug-hole, leaving a sparkling-clean new idea behind in the tub. The plucky little girl had made a stand! "We won't surrender!" she cried. "We will hide from the enemy." A flash of courage entered each one of them. "Yes! What a great idea! Where should we hide?" "In the kitchen." said Ingrid, "In the store-room. It's big enough for keeping sacks of flour, potatoes and crates of fruits from the orchard, we should make a hiding place there." The idea was no sooner suggested than adopted. All four nodded in agreement and all four scrambled to their feet and headed for the kitchen. It was now mid-afternoon and the lack of lunch was already being prodded in their minds by their empty stomachs. When they arrived in the kitchen they looked everywhere for some form of sustenance to take into the store-room for the night.

They found stale bread, some boiled turnips and potatoes – presumably cooked by Magd that morning in case lunch was allowed – and a bowl of hard-boiled eggs. A feast indeed. The food was carried into the store-room and placed on a shelf, then draped with a muslin cloth.

In the meantime, Fraulein Werner went to fetch blankets from the nearest dormitory, Winter was approaching early that year, and the nights were getting very cold. The girls got busy filling empty milk churns with water. They all knew what it was like to need precious water; they had been deprived of it enough times to value it above everything, including food!

When Fraulein Werner arrived back in the kitchen, her arms loaded with blankets, they all set to, and began to create a makeshift hiding place. Dragging crates into the middle of the store-room, which was long and narrow, and then piling sacks and bags of grain atop the crates, they were able to form a hiding place behind the improvised 'wall.' It was a crude attempt as a hideaway, but way better than being exposed and openly waiting to be captured by the Russians.

While they were lifting and dragging the heavy crates and sacks, Fraulein Werner breathlessly told the girls she had gone to Gerde Schmidt's office on her way back to the kitchen. "I told her how many people were now left in the school, just the five of us; and I told her we were planning to hide. I asked her if she wanted to join us and she refused." Ruth breathed a sigh of relief. Gerde Schmidt was not a woman to be trusted, especially when she was backed into a corner. "Did you tell her where we are hiding?" asked Ruth. "No, I led her to believe we were going to the stables." rejoined Fraulein Werner," "She was adamant that our own troops would soon come to save her, and she had already taken some blankets and food from the kitchen. She didn't seem to care about what happened to us, so I decided to keep our hiding place to myself." The poor woman looked so guilty and flustered when she finished explaining, that Ruth tried to set her mind at rest.

"Fraulein Werner, I think you did the right thing. If the enemy troops come here first and find Frau Schmidt, they might do anything to pressure her for information. If she doesn't know where we're hiding it will give us a better chance to escape." The girls both nodded in agreement. "Yes, you are right," Fraulein Werner replied, "but I just felt I should give her a better place to hide. Her office is just off the main lobby and very exposed." "Well, maybe she is correct and our own soldiers will get here first," Helga piped up, "after all, they used this school as one of their headquarters for important meetings. Surely they would want to defend it." "You are very smart to suppose this," said Fraulein Werner, "this is exactly what Frau Schmidt and I believe. We must have faith that our German boys will be the first to find us." The girls fervently nodded in agreement, and that night, when they were all wrapped in blankets in the back of the store-room, their stomachs satisfied with the vegetables and eggs, they all said a little prayer.

It was approaching dawn when they were awakened to the sound of vehicles close to the building. It was a shock to hear that sound, because the entire area had been warned not to drive anywhere during the day because they would be observed. Fraulein Werner scrambled to her feet and said she was going to see what was happening. She was still, clearly the person in charge, and anxious to regain her authority over the girls.

She headed for the Instructors Living Room, where the view was unobstructed. It was a little while before she returned, time enough for the girls to start getting anxious. When she finally came through the door into the kitchen she had a puzzled look on her face. "What did you see, Fraulein?" the girls chorused, "Who is there? What's happening?" "It's quite odd, I don't exactly know." She said, "There are several vehicles in the distance at the end of the drive and it looked like some people doing surveillance, holding binoculars; but also in the distance I saw a woman in some kind of uniform and a heavy coat. It looks like she's walking towards the front entrance." "Do you think it's the Russian Army?" wailed Helga, "What should we do?" All of the night before, the four of them had been tense, sleeping fitfully, building up nervousness. "I don't think so," said Fraulein Werner, and the three girls relaxed a little, "but I'm not sure. I didn't recognize the color of the vehicles."

"Can we go and look?" asked Ruth "Perhaps we can recognize them." Fraulein Werner looked up in astonishment. "You?" she said, "How would you girls know?" "Because once a month Frau Schmidt gave us a special class learning all the insignia and colors of different Military Ranks in different countries. It was part of our training to always recognize a threat. Maybe if we had a look we could tell you who is there and we'd know what to expect, how to prepare." "Fraulein Lindenau, your idea makes sense," the Instructor responded. "We will all go together as quickly as we can, to ascertain the situation." She needed to say nothing more. The girls ran willingly to the kitchen door and waited for their Instructor to lead the way. Once at the window in the Instructor's Living Room, all four of them craned their necks to the left, to see who was at the top of the driveway. They were concentrating so much on the distant vehicles, that they didn't see the woman standing right near the steps leading up to the front door.

"Ach, du Lieber Himmel!" Oh! Good Heavens! Shouted Helga and Ruth at the same time, "Those are Red Cross vehicles, not military ones!" They were just drinking in that piece of good news when Helga gave an ear-splitting scream! "Oh, mein Gott, mein Gott! Das ist meine Schwester!" "What!" chorused the others, your Sister?" "Yes!" cried Helga, dancing around in elated circles, tears streaming down her face, "She was a Nurse in Danzig. Now it looks like she joined the Red Cross!" All three girls joined Helga in her delirious dance, shrieking and whooping their happiness out loud. It was the first time in three years they had released feelings like this, and once discovered it was hard to stop. It was intoxicating! But stop they did!

The door to the room burst open and a furious Frau Schmidt strode toward them, blowing a whistle and waving her arms about in fury. "How dare you scream! She roared. "Halt deinen Munds!" Shut your mouths! Everyone froze, even Fraulein Werner. "Was machs du?" What are you doing? "We are at war, not on vacation!" Frau Schmidt had never looked more incensed. The girls bowed their heads in instant supplication, but Fraulein Werner raised her head courageously and told Gerde Schmidt that the Red Cross were in the Munster Walde grounds. Frau Schmidt had barely a minute to absorb the information when a loud banging at the front door could clearly be heard, coupled with the sound of a bell being rung inside the building. "Stay here!" Commanded Frau Schmidt, and she marched out of the room the girls knew she was headed for the front door. They followed her; a respectful distance behind. No longer as intimidated by the bullying woman as they had been.

When the door opened and Helga's sister appeared, she stepped immediately into the hall. "Frau Schmidt?" she enquired. "I am she."

replied the Instructor. "I am Charlotte Vogel, and I'm here to take all the girls you have on these premises into safe keeping." "That is not possible!" shouted Frau Schmidt, "I will call the local police! I am responsible for these girls and I cannot allow you to take them!" Helga ran over to her sister and threw her arms around her in a gripping hug. "Charlotte, there are only three of us girls left here. All the others have already escaped!"

Still, at this final hour, Frau Schmidt was truly propagandized, only able to repeat the information with which she had been indoctrinated. "You can do whatever you please, Fraulein, "Just understand that you will suffer for this, and the girls must remain here." Grabbing Helga's hand and nodding toward Ruth and Ingrid, Charlotte eyed Frau Schmidt with a look of disdain, and walking to the open front door with the girls in tow, she turned and faced the two shocked Instructors. "They go with me," she said, simply, "Come!". And the four of them walked, the girls in absolute wonderment, to the waiting vehicles at the top of the driveway.

Several vehicles were parked there. The officials giving orders to the Red Cross had anticipated many more girls needing to be rescued. Men in heavy coats were walking around, stamping their feet and rubbing their hands together; wisps of condensation escaping from their mouths in the cold air. Ruth was overwhelmed. None of this felt real. She took Ingrid's hands in hers, and laughing and crying at the same time, all she could think of, all she could say, over and over, "Wir sind frei! Wir sind frei!" We're free! We're free! "Wir gehen nach Hause! Wir gehen nach hause!" We're going home! We're going home!

Charlotte eventually came up and told them that Helga was going home with her, and that the two of them, Ruth and Ingrid, would be taken to Elbing, a village about 20 kilometers from Ingrid's town in the South, and 32 kilometers from Tiegenort where Ruth had lived. The two girls thanked everyone profusely for coming to their rescue, and climbed gladly into the truck which was indicated to drive them home. Along the way, there were troubling signs of people leaving the area, and by the time they arrived at Elbing both girls were afraid of what they might find when they reached their villages.

Ruth was very familiar with Elbing. She had cycled there a few times with Brigitte, just to look in the shop windows and buy some cookies, and she recalled it had taken them about an hour and a half from Tiegenort.

She reasoned that if the bicycle ride took that amount of time, it would probably be a five hour walk, but she was so excited to be almost home the notion didn't daunt her. After all, the Instructors at Munster Walde had made certain that all the girls could hike 50 kilometers with hardly any food and water!

Ingrid knew the town even better. Her mother's friend, Katya, lived there, and she had visited many times to play with Katya's son, Markus. Ingrid was fairly certain that Katya was still living there as her whole family also lived in Elbing. Ingrid, always the plucky, independent little girl, had no problem telling Ruth to begin her walk home. They had become fast friends and they had no intention of losing touch with one another. Ruth set off walking on the road to Tiegenort. Her eyes were tearing up from happiness so often, that she sometimes had to stop and wipe them on the corner of the blanket, given her by the Red Cross, she had draped around her shoulders. She was empty-handed and freezing cold, but her shoes were sturdy and she was ready for the long walk home.

After an hour or so, she heard the clip-clop, clip-clop of a horses hooves, and turning around she saw a smartly-dressed gentleman driving a horse-drawn cart. As he approached her he brought the horse to a slow trot and leaned over towards her to talk. "Good afternoon, Fraulein," he said, "where are you heading for?" as Ruth walked up closer to the cart and looked him in the eye, his eyes opened up in astonishment. He had recognized those green eyes and that copper-colored hair! "Oh, my God, do my eyes deceive me? Are you Augusta Lindenau's child?" "Yes, that's me," replied Ruth, and you are Herr Walter Krause I believe?" "Yes, yes, dear child, I am he. But what are you doing walking the street at this time of day and in this bitter cold?"

"It's a long story, Herr Krause. I've been away for three years and I have managed to escape from hell. Now all I want is to get home to my family." The horse was pulled to a stop and Herr Krause jumped down to the road. Taking Ruth into his arms he lifted her on to the cart, wrapped a blanket around her entire body and took her home to Tiegenort.

When Augusta opened the door to the sound of Ruth's knocking, she almost fainted on the doorstep, but Herr Krause held both women up. "Mutti, Mutti," said Ruth, "Ich bin frei! Ich bin frei!" I'm free, I'm free!

Looking back, it was a bittersweet day. Upon entering the home Ruth was surprised to see her sister living there again; but this time with a little four-year-old girl, Magrid. Within twenty four hours Ruth's Father would return to the home also, but now the family was shrouded with fear. Her father said that the German soldiers no longer had guns, so the officers gave the lower ranks shovels to protect themselves as they fled. Within another twenty four hours the whole village was evacuated by the German Army's Headquarters, and told to go to the Baltic coast where a German Freighter would rescue them.

Ruth's freedom was short-lived.

Chapter Seventeen

Her village was being evacuated! The Russian Army was fast approaching; pushing the German Army as hard as they could. The best that could be done by the German military was to breach both Dams on the two Rivers, the Weichsel and the Tiege, in order to flood the village and allow the fleeing soldiers and civilians to escape. If they could get to the coastline before it flooded everywhere, they would all have a chance to escape. Ruth's family were panic-stricken! Everyone in Tiegenort had been told to leave immediately they got notice to do so. There was no chance to do anything except to pack up as many precious possessions as they could carry.

In Ruth's case it was her shiny riding boots and brown tweed britches, both of them her pride and joy. She also took sheet music and some favorite books and trinkets. Since her absence of three years she had grown out of most clothing remaining in her closet, but she took a couple of long skirts and a knitted shawl which she had worn on Winter sleigh-rides. Her parents packed all they could, all they considered important, into two trunks and loaded everything onto a wheelbarrow.

It was early on a bitterly cold morning that Ruth and her parents said goodbye to their home. As they closed the door and looked down the street, all their neighbors were doing the same thing; fleeing for their lives! Men and women, young and old, and children. The weak, the strong and the disabled; all were heading for the marshy lands which would take them to the coast and, hopefully, to the ship which would come to rescue them. It was a long walk, but fortunately the ground was so cold and frozen that everyone could walk on the marsh-land without getting their feet soaking wet; but it was an arduous journey for the aged and infirm – many of them soldiers who had suffered injuries.

The walk lasted six hours, and when they reached the coast everyone collapsed in relief. From this time on in their lives, nobody knew what was going to happen. The winter was, by now, so harsh that the sea was frozen close to the coast. Older, local people had seen this before, but everyone was now concerned that the rescue ships would not be able to come into the port. Everything in their lives was now uncertain.

The two ships which had been ordered to pick them all up were delayed. The ocean had frozen over and the Captains were nervous about getting into the port. Of course, the people on the shore were not aware of this, so all they could do was wait. In the end, the ships were ordered to maneuver as close as they could to the shore, and by two o'clock the next morning it was time to get aboard the ships. Everyone had to walk and slip across the frozen water in the darkness until they reached the ships, and when they finally grasped the roped gangway they were shocked to see the vessels were both rusty old freighters which looked barely seaworthy. But if this was their only means of escape they weren't complaining.

They were all sent down to the hold in the ships, and packed in, as Ruth recalled, just like sardines in a can. For three days and nights they stayed in this situation, floating in the middle of the Baltic Sea. Almost no food, just stale sea biscuits. No facilities for washing or defecating. Everything done in full view of everyone else. They were told eventually that they were to be transferred to other ships bound for Denmark. One of the last ships to pick up refugees, which included Ruth's aunt and her four children, was named Gustloff. They had barely left the Port when a Russian plane flew over and bombed the ship, killing everyone on board.

Several ships passed by, all at sinking point with war-wounded and refugees; but eventually a ship passed them and sent a message they had room for the refugees. Everyone climbed the makeshift gangway on to the Danish ship and mentally prepared, from that moment on, to be homeless.

It didn't take long to arrive in Denmark, a day or two at most, and then the grueling task of rounding everyone up began. Across the country there were over 1,000 small locations designated to house the huge influx of people. Much to the resentment of the Danish people, schools, factories, hotels, assembly houses and sports facilities were all seized by the German authorities and designated as housing for the refugees, approximately 250,000 of them by Wars end. Many of the refugees were women, children and elderly, with a high proportion of children under the age of fifteen, and many of them were sick and malnourished. On disembarking from the ships, the enormous groups were escorted by armed guards to warehouses on the Dock, where they were ushered into a vast space, already occupied by hundreds of refugees who had come into the port on other ships. Throughout the day, groups of people were gathered into transportable numbers and then escorted to military trucks which would take them to their destinations. On the whole, family members were allowed to be together, but it was an understandably haphazard system which sometimes meant that families were separated.

Ruth's family was torn. She, her sister Gertrude with her daughter Magrid and her parents were together, which was good; but the worst part of the equation was that her grandparents were not with them, and they had no idea where they were. Eventually, their group was called to be transported and after a long drive they arrived at the place which was to be their 'home.'

It was in Odense. The building was an old school. The majority of rooms were small classrooms, though there was a large room with a stage which, presumably, had been used as an Assembly Hall, and this was the place to which all the prisoners were taken when they arrived. There were no chairs, so everyone eventually sat on the floor, as there was a long wait. Every person was obliged to give their name and supply paper identification. Of course many people had no other identification than knowing their name and where they had come from, so the process took the whole day. To add to the confusion, not many Danish people spoke German, so there was a very limited number of people doing this 'registration process.' When it was the turn of Ruth's parents they fortunately had enough identification with them to satisfy the authorities.

Striding around the Hall was a tall, slim, blonde man in Danish Military uniform. He was carrying sheaves of papers and marking them periodically. He looked a little overwhelmed at times, and then another Danish uniformed man stepped up to help him. The two men were giving orders to other uniformed men, and after some hours of watching it became clear to most people that they were the Commander of the school and his second in command. He did not make himself known to anyone, just supervised the work being done by the people admitting all the refugees.

Eventually, Ruth's family was escorted to a room on the second floor of the school; Room No 9. It was a small room, formerly a classroom. The guard indicated they should enter, and when the four were inside, the heavy sound of a bolt being closed could be heard. Ruth and her family looked around. On the floor straw was scattered around and there were a couple of bales against a wall. Sitting about on the straw were 8 people, all of them hugging their belongings and looking fearful and anxious. With the arrival of Ruth's family it would seem that the room was now filled to capacity, so everyone shuffled about until there was a fairly equal amount of space for each person and their precious belongings.

In the corner of the room there was a small table holding a large metal pitcher containing water. Beside the pitcher were half a dozen metal mugs, clearly to be shared. Most of the people in the room had brought shawls and blankets and they were huddling together to keep warm since the temperature in the room was frigid. Friends, families or strangers, it didn't matter; in that perishing room survival was the uppermost thought. There were windows in the room, but they were small, high up and heavily barred.

Ruth and her family settled as best they could, and their room-mates watched them without interfering. The noises outside the room were quite upsetting. A woman wailing; a guard shouting orders; children crying and the slamming of doors. Everyone in the room recognized the sounds which confirmed they were now detainees with absolutely no rights, and every heart was afraid and wondering what their fate might be. After a while, one of the men broke the ice and introduced himself and his wife, Freidrich and Thea Lange, from Berlin. That started a domino effect, and everyone in turn quietly made themselves known and where they were from. A widow, Sophia Kholer and her daughter, Margot and a family of four, a husband, wife and two teenaged sons, both of whom were nursing serious injuries. Ruth remembered them only as the Vogel's. They kept very much to themselves. Not unfriendly, but always occupied taking care of their sons; always worried, always fretful about one boy or another.

Occasionally, the sound of something banging against their windows caused them to raise their heads toward the sounds, and sometimes whatever was being thrown, stuck to the glass and slid down, leaving a dark streak. The man who had first introduced himself, Freidrich Lange, who sported a handlebar mustache which seemed to match his outgoing character, was the tallest man in the room, so he went to see what was happening. He moved the small table under the windows, and climbed up to look. "Ach, mein Gott." Oh, my God! "The street below is crowded with people," he said emotionally, "and they are all throwing vegetables and rocks at the building and shouting, Mordere! Mordere!" "What does that mean?" asked his wife, Thea. Freidrich spoke some Danish having traveled to Denmark many times before the war. "It means Murderers." He said to everyone. "The reality is we are all here as prisoners in Denmark, not refugees" he said, jumping down from the table, "and we must be prepared to be despised and hated! Despised and hated!" His stance and voice were both hinting on the theatrical, so everyone took a deep breath to consider his words; but his expression was deadly serious as he sank back down on the straw and hung his head in humiliation.

It took a while for the really quite obvious fact to sink in. So many of the West Prussians, especially, had been burying their heads in the sand that they didn't want to acknowledge what had been going on around them. Or at least, they knew but they didn't want any part of it. Their lives in that part of the world had been settled and happy. When all hell broke loose around them, many, though not all of them, tried to go on living as before.

Well, now it was all too late. Though officially they were designated as refugees, they were treated as prisoners of war, and whatever was going to happen in their futures was not in their hands. Every day, day in, day out, in the little schoolroom, the group of thirteen people became friends. Or at least they became closer and closer. Ruth's father, who had not been well since they left Tiegenort, was pining for his life as a mail-man. He wore his uniform mail-man hat every day, probably just as a way to remind himself of his past happy life.

Freidrich and Thea Lange quickly became the couple in the room who kept up the other's spirits. They were from Berlin, where they had owned and run a Theater, and they had a wealth of entertaining stories to tell, which helped to pass the endless hours of boredom during the first months of confinement. When Danish people walking below their windows yelled out obscenities, Freidrich would be the first one to tell a joke, or spin one of his anecdotes. He tended to repeat himself, as if once making a statement he liked, he would say it again.

One woman in the room, Sophia Kohler, who had been widowed a year before, was there with her daughter, Margot. She was a sweet lady with a gentle disposition, and she made a special friendship with Augusta, Ruth's mother, who was about the same age. She had been a seamstress in a clothing factory, making uniforms for the German military. In turn, Margot and Ruth became friends. The two girls had a lot in common with one another. Margot loved to dance; she had been taking extra classes and had practiced at home for hours every day. Her dream had been to be a ballerina, but the war put a stop to all her visions of going to Russia and learning with the Bolshoi Academy. She and Ruth talked for hours about their disappointments and their hopes. Ruth understood her very well, as she had also wanted to take her singing and piano playing to a professional level, performing on stage to an ecstatic audience.

In the room that became home, after a few weeks Ruth and her family, along with their fellow room-mates, were beginning to understand the rules and regulations of their confinement. Every morning and evening one person from each room had to re-fill the water pitcher. Water was obtained from a faucet in the back yard of the school, and the person who fetched the water was observed at all times. At 7 AM each day, two large bowls of gruel, a concoction of rye flour or wheat boiled in water was brought to them. The mixture was too thin to be eaten with a spoon, so everyone took turns with the metal mugs and drank their meagre share. Later in the day, if they were lucky, they got some bread, usually stale, and some kind of soup.

They all experienced soup made of vegetable peelings with razor blades hidden in its depths. They all experienced food tasting like nothing they had tasted before. Who knew? Dog? Cat? Rat? They could only speculate. They all also experienced being robbed! The unpopular job of being a guard for the refugees made it difficult for the authorities to find people of the best character. They needed hundreds of people across the country to perform this task, and many civilians who were given the job had ulterior motives. Some wanted to harm the refugees and others wanted to steal from them. The night-time guards were the worst. When all was locked and silent in the building, the night-time guards would go around the rooms in pairs. Their aim was to get in and out of a room as quickly as possible. Once inside the room and the door closed, one guard would brandish threateningly a gun or a knife, and the other guard would go to two or three of the refugees belongings and rifle through them, looking for valuables. Since valuables were pretty much all the refugees brought with them, there was a lot of booty to be found. Especially jewelry. If someone screamed loud enough when their bundles were robbed, and if enough fuss was made that the Danish military, always on the premises, heard the commotion, then the guards would be punished and the items returned; but mostly, with a weapon waved in their faces, the refugees kept their mouths shut and the guards got away with their crime. It became very clear, very quickly, that the Danes were not happy to be hosting these fugitives.

One night, when this situation happened, the target was the room holding Ruth's family. The usual scenario happened. As soon as the door creaked open Ruth was wide awake! She nudged Margot who was sleeping next to her, and put her finger to her lips, pointing to the two dark shadows moving about in the room. To her horror one shadow moved to her bundle of treasures and began rifling around in it. The second shadow went to Margot's box. The two girls had very little, but their ultimate treasures were, for Ruth, her riding boots, and for Margot her ballet slippers. The girls both let out a scream and, within seconds, a knife was put to Ruth's neck. Boots and ballet slippers were taken; along with Ruth's riding breeches and Margot's silver Christening bracelet.

The next morning, after a totally sleepless night, Ruth asked to see the Commander of the school. His name was Commander Andersson. She had to wait for a week until her request was granted, but on the day she had her appointment her anger and resentment was still overpowering. She strode into the Commander's office at the appointed time, and spoke on behalf of Margo, as well as herself. Well, she tried to speak. Her knowledge of Danish was close to zero and the 'German Interpreter' who was called into the office to help her, had very little knowledge of German. The Commander himself was quite an imposing figure. She recognized him as the tall, imposing man she had seen before in the large Assembly Hall, on the day they had all arrived at the school. He was tall and handsome, with blonde hair and a slightly grim look on his face, which actually enhanced his looks. All military personnel who represented the Danish Government were thoroughly vetted for their jobs. Too many German sympathizers and Communists remained in Denmark, and the Government and Danish people, at that stage of the war had all had enough. At that time, in the Assembly Hall, he had seemed overwhelmed with the large influx of refugees, and quite brittle when he gave orders, but on this occasion in his office, he had clearly got a grip on his job and was calm and considerate. This was only a body-language impression Ruth got. After all he spoke no German, but it looked as though he was trying to understand. In the end, after a struggle with the interpreter, Ruth asked in sign language for pen and paper. The penny dropped! Paper and pen were supplied and Ruth drew a very good depiction of a guard, a pair of riding boots and a pair of ballet slippers. The interpreter and the Commander gazed at the picture and smiled; nodding their heads and indicating they understood. Ruth was ecstatic. The interpreter left the office and a few moments later he returned, holding a pair of ballet slippers, a huge smile on his face. Ruth pointed to the sketch of her riding boots. The interpreter shook his head, looking gloomy. The ballet slippers had been thrown away in a corridor when the thieving guards absconded. They were worth nothing. The beautiful leather boots, however, were another story.

The next interaction Ruth's family had with the Authorities overseeing the detainees occurred two or three months after they arrived. And of all strange things, it was connected to the hat Fritz, her father wore. It had taken several weeks for the paperwork of each family to be scrutinized and accepted. The Danish Authorities were seeking out declared communists and politically active Danish citizens who frequently hid amongst the German refugees, so verifying everybody's papers was quite an arduous task. Perhaps it should be stated here that at the beginning of the war, Denmark had declared itself impartial, and allowed Germany to use their country in any way they saw fit. As the war progressed, the Danish people revolted, and caused almost a revolution, which became an enormous movement in 1945 when the war ended and Germany capitulated.

Many Danes were appalled by the atrocities performed by Hitler's Armies, and they wanted nothing to do with harboring German refugees. One Danish guard took a close look at Fritz's post-man's hat and declared it was suspicious. The writing on the hat was not understood by the Danish guard and he was determined to find Fritz guilty of something! Day after day Fritz was taken into an interrogation room and questioned as to his affiliation, and try as he might, nobody believed it was simply the insignia of the German Post Office. When, one day the guard threatened Fritz that he was to be sent away to another camp with hard labor, Ruth's sister, Gertrude, who was a beauty and not afraid of anyone, made it her business to cozy up to him, letting him know who her father was. The guard was quickly bowled over by Gertrude's charms. The deportation of Fritz was put on hold, and over a few days the guard was willing to believe everything Gertrude said. She implored Ruth one day to go with her when her father was again going to be interrogated. The two sisters knew what they had to do, and as it happened the story was absolutely true. Their father had been a mail-man in West Prussia, and he simply loved his hat! It wasn't clear if the sisters won the argument with their charms, or if it was discovered in some form of research, but after the two sisters pled for their father, Fritz was allowed to wear his hat with no repercussions for as long as he remained in the school.

Ruth's sister, Gertrude, had left the family home in Tiegenort when she was seventeen. She was a young, stunning beauty, who wanted to go on the stage, and nothing was going to stop her. She found her way to

Berlin and did a little acting, but rumors of War abounded, and finding work or even getting experience in that field was almost impossible. Eventually, after the war, she landed a role in the original movie 'Titanic', having never given up her dream; but in Berlin, at that time, she had to take any opportunity that came along. In 1939, Ruth thought, Gertrude met a man much older than she. He was a Barber who owned a store and at the age of 18 she became pregnant with his child. Her parents, Fritz and Augusta persuaded her to marry him as he would offer her some stability. She did marry him and stayed with him for a while, but in less than a year the Russian Army advanced on Berlin; they raided all the German-owned businesses and threw out the owners, Gertrude and her husband included. Her husband was recruited into the German Army and it's unclear whether or not he perished, but Gertrude, at some point, obtained a Divorce after having been married for two years. Pregnant Gertrude fled back to Tiegenort and her parent's home, where she gave birth to a daughter, naming her Magrid. Gertrude was not the most devoted mother in the world, certainly at that time, so it fell to her mother and father to take care of the parenting. Ruth was at the Munster Walde School during this time, and she didn't see her sister or niece until she herself escaped and went home. Ironically, the little family had just a few short days together before ending up on the ship carrying them all, and thousands of others, to Denmark.

After Ruth and her family had been refugees in Odense for about three months, Christmas time came around. The Danish Authorities knew that Christmas, "Weinachten," was an important holiday for the German people, so they gave permission on Christmas Eve for the refugees to go to Midnight Mass. Through Ruth's eyes it was a huge shock! She recalled everyone in the school being allowed out of the building, and on the streets for the first time since they arrived. They were all formed into lines of four people per line, and ended up as a long line of people four people wide. Then they were escorted to the Church. Guards holding guns escorted them. Danish people in the street yelled obscenities at them as they walked towards the Church. At the church, the refugees were directed to sit in all the pews at the back, and they did not receive communion. Ruth was stunned! "They treated us like prisoners," she said. "The Danish treated us like criminals!" At this late hour, Ruth, who had herself suffered at the hands of the Germans, it would seem still didn't precisely understand what her countrymen had done.

Chapter Eighteen

As soon as Gertrude realized she had some persuasive powers with the authorities in the school, she made it her business to try and discover where Augusta's mother, Anna Lindenau, was being held. Coupled with the Danish Authorities, the Red Cross had been busy documenting names at the numerous makeshift camps all over Denmark in an effort to try and bring families together. Thousands of people were looking for relatives and loved ones, so the task was daunting to say the least. Gertrude tried every day to get permission to speak with the person who was overseeing the inhabitants of the school, the second in command, Captain Bjorn Jensen. She told her parents that she believed keeping their Grandmother's name constantly on the list might find her faster than others, whose families might only make a single enquiry. In fact, that might well have been her belief, but she knew soon enough, from experience, that the Captain was more than a little attracted to her. She played the game and pretended she didn't know, just flashed him innocent looks when she saw him almost every day. Over the weeks and months, she got to know this man rather well. All her energies were directed at seducing him and it didn't take long. Gertrude had regained 'her power'.

As the months rolled by, and people around the world got used to the fact that the war was over, they became aware of the huge humanitarian quandary that Denmark was dealing with. The United States were particularly helpful. Groups of people all over the country began sending 'Care Packages' to the German refugees. People donated everything from knitting yarn and bolts of fabric to books, cans of food, medicines and stationary. It was clear that at some point all these detainees would have to be repatriated back to their country of origin, and it was believed that sending practical items to them while they waited, would give them a chance to return to a semblance of normalcy.

Suddenly, the diets of everyone improved. The canned foods were a very welcome supplement to the sparse and meagre food of earlier times. Augusta was delighted when yarn and knitting needles were made available. She loved to knit, and that simple pleasure brought her hours of contentment as she made socks and scarves to keep her family warm, and sweaters and hats; the possibilities were endless, and Augusta threw herself into her hobby with great enthusiasm. Ruth watched her mother and also learned how to knit. Even little Margot was shown the skill, and it kept her happy at her grandmother's knee. It was a hobby that remained with Ruth for her entire life, and even helped her create a business many years later. Her father, Fritz, although a Mailman in Tiegenort, was also a skilled Tailor. He had learned the profession as a young man from his Father, so he was now able to make jackets and coats for people in the camp who needed them; and for payment he received extra food rations for his family.

The more the lives of the refugees were taken into consideration, and goods and supplies for them from around the world began to pour into Denmark, the more stringent rules in the encampments were relaxed. Two large Camps were built in Oksbol, near the Danish North Sea, and accommodated 37,000 refugees, and in Klovermarken near Copenhagen, which housed 19,000 people, these camps included such things as schools and medical facilities. The lack of which had been putting a huge strain on the Danish authorities. Thousands of children who should be attending school, and thousands of aged and infirm who needed constant attention, could soon be taken care of, if only in a basic way, and very basic it was. Most of the sick people who were taken care of, were those who had communicable diseases which could be passed on the Danish guards.

In the school in Odense where Ruth and her family were housed, the relaxation of rules also applied. Children were allowed into the large Assembly Hall and taught basic learning skills, though it was still very difficult finding people who were willing to teach them. Mostly, it was the German refugees themselves who volunteered to school the children. Adults were given books, canvases, paints and brushes. People began to fill their days with hobbies and crafts. As time went by, an opportunity came to the little group in Room 9 which kept most of them so busy there were barely enough hours in the day!

At the suggestion of the Danish government, by late Springtime small detention centers around the country had been given permission to organize a Summer Show of sorts. A theatrical presentation where the detainees could be kept busy and occupied organizing and writing their own styles of entertainment for the detainees who were either unable or unwilling to perform on a stage.

The second military person in command of their school, Captain Bjorn Jensen, Gertrude's blossoming friend, was in charge of the entire project. He knew that the Lange's in Room 9 had been Theater owners, so he asked them if they would be willing to 'Put on a Show.' They were ecstatic! Freidrich could finally put his comedic writing skills, and his memory, to the test, and Thea could audition people with talent to take part in the show and work on the organizational side. They didn't have too far to look for the first formation of the production. Freidrich asked Augusta and Sophia if they would be willing to make costumes for the performers, and both ladies willingly agreed. "I will go and ask if we can have a sewing machine in our room," Thea said, "then we can make a lot more things. I will also find some more ladies to help with making the costumes, I've seen quite a few ladies making clothes in the hobbies room." The authorities had designated a hobbies room on the ground floor of the school when supplies began coming in from around the world, and there were several sewing machines housed there. Some of them very old, to be sure, but at least they worked! In that same room were numerous bolts of fabric, designated for the refugees to make their own clothes, which they did, but a lot of the fabrics were not suitable for clothing; too bold in design, too flimsy, too heavy, and so on. These fabrics were perfect for turning into costumes and stage props.

Ruth and Margot were beside themselves, showing great interest in everything being discussed. "I can perform some ballet recitals, now that I have my shoes back." Margot squealed. " I can remember all of the ones I learned." "I'll play the music for you ," said Ruth, "and I have some of my favorite sheet music which I brought from home, so I can play a piano solo. I can also sing, if you want, Herr Lange." she said with a little smile, batting her eyes at him. "Oh, Fraulein," he retorted sagely, "you have no idea! No idea at all!" And a huge smile broke out on his handsome, mustached face.

Frau Vogel, the usually very quiet lady, told the group she was also eager to help with whatever they would need, and then she surprised everyone, "I used to make parachutes and worked on large tarpaulins in a factory," she said proudly, "I can make curtains and backdrops for the stage." Then turning to her husband she nudged him and nodded her head, "Yes, yes," said Herr Vogel, "I am a carpenter, "I can help with the stage sets."

This wonderful offer was accepted with enormous enthusiasm, and within a few days, sewing, sketching designs and writing skits was underway. Down in the hobbies room, Thea unearthed an ancient gramophone with a horn and a box of old records, which would be a brilliant prop for their parodies. A rather musty out-of-tune piano was unearthed from under an oilcloth in a storage shed in the back yard. Owned originally by the school, it was discarded and left when the German army took over the building. Carried in by four or five male refugees, it was carefully placed in the hobbies room for anyone who needed it, to practice for the Show. Thea found a person who knew how to tune it, and a schedule was drawn up for people who needed to use it; and it turned out to be a surprising number of people.

Another piano was in the Assembly Hall. Covered over with heavy blankets, nobody had seen it or heard it play in four or five years. Then one day when Ruth and Margot were in the hobbies room – Ruth playing the piano for Margot while she practiced her ballet routines – Freidrich Lange walked into the room to search for some fabric suitable to upholster a stool. It was the first time he had heard Ruth play the piano. He walked right past her while she played, then turned around and sat down on a chair to watch her. He was transfixed! Poor Margot danced away, doing her pirouettes and pas de chat; doing them beautifully, but Freidrich was focusing entirely on Ruth and her playing. When the piece was over and Freidrich 'came to,' he was smart enough to praise Margot first. "You were wonderful, my dear Fraulein," he gushed, "wonderful! We will have some beautiful cameos for you in the Show." As Margot blushed and pirouetted some more, Freidrich walked over to Ruth and bent down to whisper in her ear. "Fraulein Lindenau, I had heard from your parents that you were good, but you are exceptional! Exceptional" Ruth was, of course, delighted, saying "Thank you so much Herr Lange, I'm so glad you like my playing." "Fraulein Lindenau," Freidrich continued, "do you also play classical pieces?" "Yes, of course, Herr Lange," Ruth replied, "Which ones in particular do you like?" "Oh, any and all, Fraulein." was his reply, "Any and all." "Then I should be happy to play you a small recital." Said Ruth, and she lifted her hands above the keyboard to prepare. "No! No!" Shouted Herr Lange. "Not here! I shall get permission from the Commander to allow you to play the Grand Piano in the Assembly Hall. You need a magnificent instrument, and I shall ask if we may use it in the Summer Show, and if you may practice on it!" Ruth was overjoyed! Her years of hard work practicing, and her dreams of playing to an audience, albeit an audience of German refugees, was finally coming to pass.

Within a few days the permission was granted. Thea asked the piano-tuner to do his very best, and Ruth was soon allowed to go down to the Assembly Hall to practice her classical presentation. For some reason she was quite nervous the first time she went. Her mother had been knitting up a storm lately, and she had made a green sweater in fine wool, with short sleeves and a ribbed waistband. It perfectly matched Ruth's green eyes. Ruth decided to wear it for her practice, with a cream skirt which skimmed her ankles, made by Sophia; her mother and friend had performed a miracle! Clothes like this were a whole world away. She felt fabulous! And with her red wavy hair worn loose, she looked fabulous. At age seventeen, almost eighteen, her life was just beginning.

She went down to the first floor and entered the Assembly Hall, knees knocking. At the entrance, a Danish guard nodded to her and entered with her. Even in here she was being guarded. Bearing in mind that Ruth had been indoctrinated to be tough and resilient in Munster Walde, she was still a mixture of both worlds. She felt a huge resentment that her people were being treated in a similar way to the way she had been treated as a thirteen, fourteen, fifteen and sixteen year-old, but her character had been hardened, though her spirit was never squashed. She was used to being treated with disdain by her own people, so this was not too different. The only change in dynamics, was that she had begun to understand the power of her own femininity. Just like her sister Gertrude.

She entered the Assembly Hall with sheet music clutched in her hand, and walked toward the magnificent Grand Piano, which had been polished and tuned to perfection. Sitting at the stool, a frisson of fear went through her body, but as soon as her hands touched the ivory keys she was transported into her own world where everything was beautiful and nothing ugly existed.

She played Mozart, she played Beethoven, she played Bruch and Debussy. It was a joyful time for her; the first time she had played classical music in over a year. She had been given an hour and a half to practice on that day and she filled every minute, hardly pausing to rest her hands. Halfway through, Commander Andersson heard the sound from an outside hallway. He opened the door to the Assembly Hall and entered. When he saw who was playing he closed the door and just stood there listening, next to the guard, frozen to the spot. Ruth did not know he was there. When she was finished, she stood up, quietly closed the lid on the piano and walked towards the door. He was no longer there.

Room No 9 was a hive of industry. Freidrich and Thea Lange had recalled several burlesque sequels from their days in the Theatre, and were kept busy making copious notes and adapting the skits to the talents and capabilities of the volunteer performers. Once they knew that part of the plan they could put people to work making the costumes. Freidrich had already in his mind several roles for Ruth. She would play a classical solo. She would accompany Margot with her ballet recitals and she would play piano when the burlesque scenes were performed. On top of that, she would sing! He envisioned her singing both patriotic, classical and popular songs, but that was yet to be decided; the bottom line was that Ruth would be the star of the show!

Gertrude, ten years Ruth's senior, was not happy about this outcome. The truth of it was that Gertrude was so wrapped up in herself that she hadn't noticed her sisters blossoming looks, or shown any interest in the fact that her sister could play the piano and sing. Neither of which she could do. She did, however, know how to perform and show off her own good looks, so Freidrich had cast her in several of the skits he'd written. Thea put up a notice in the hobbies room, asking for volunteers to perform in the show; anyone with a special talent. One of the elderly refugees in the building played the violin. His own instrument had been stolen, but Gertrude asked Captain Jensen if he could obtain one for the Show and it was no sooner said than done. A lady in her late sixties had been a yodeling champion in her village, and she quickly volunteered to be one of the performers. Two couples said they would do some German Dances together, having spent years in the same village and practiced dancing every week.

Freidrich played the accordion, and he would be using that skill throughout the show. His treasured instrument had not been stolen; was still intact in its carrying bag, probably because he slept every night with it under the blankets at his feet! Two young people in their early teens, a brother and sister, offered to do a puppeteering act. They didn't have any puppets, but Augusta volunteered to make them, much to the young peoples' delight. Little Magrid got involved with her grandmother designing and making two beautiful dolls, a King and a Queen, using all the scraps of material that were left over from making larger costumes. Herr Vogel made cross-sticks, and then found some string to attach the puppets and bring them to life. Then he made a small stage for the puppeteers to hide behind. His two sons, although injured and relatively immobile, were both fine artists, and they painted beautiful designs on the mini-stage, delighting the young brother and sister. The brothers graduated to painting stage sets as well, and their talents were so admirable that Fredrich made a mental note that if he ever ended up in Berlin again, with a theatre, he would hire the two brothers on the spot!

After 12 weeks of blissful, (or so the refugees thought) designing, practicing and creating, the show was ready to be performed. There was only one fly in the ointment. Every morning for several weeks, Gertrude had been avoiding breakfast. Yet she had needed every day to go to the bathroom with her mother, who was her designated care-giver. Augusta knew within days that her daughter was pregnant, but the consequences of the pregnancy were so severe that that Augusta didn't even tell Fritz, her husband.

If the authorities had known that one of their Danish Guards had made a refugee pregnant the Guard would have been executed. Augusta told her daughter, "This is the bed you decided to lie on. Now you must suffer the consequences." Poor Augusta! Already bringing up the child of Gertrude's failed marriage, and now in a virtual prison camp with her daughter causing such humiliation she could hardly bear it.

Gertrude was quite flippant about the whole thing. As long as she could perform in the Summer Show everything would be all right. She had such a hold over the Captain that an arrangement was made. The costumes she wore in the Show would disguise her pregnancy. After the baby was born, the Captain and his wife would adopt the baby. The Captain and his wife had no options, unless they were happy he should be executed!

In the meantime, preparations for the show went at full speed ahead. It was amazing how the relatively small amount of production help was able to do so much in three short months. The Show was to be performed in late August, over a period of four days, and refugees from other small camps had been invited to come as well. Freidrich and Thea were truly professionals. They knew exactly what they were doing and how to bring the best out of the individual performers. The quiet Vogel family were a huge asset to the group, which just goes to show that still waters run deep. Between themselves, they were basically doing everything for the stage; woodwork, draperies, curtains and painting. Everyone was very proud of the Vogels when they were finished.

At about the same time as the stage was ready, costumes had also been made, rehearsals had gone well, music had been practiced. The only thing remaining was to 'Let the Show Begin!'

Chapter Nineteen

If Ruth had liked the outfit she wore to rehearsals, she loved her costumes for the performance! She had three changes. One for the classical performance, which was a long black velvet skirt and a white lace blouse. The second was for the burlesque skits when she played in accompaniment with Fredrich Lange on his Accordion and the elderly Violin player. This, according to Ruth, was the outfit she loved best because it was a combination of gold and red with ruffled sleeves and a flouncy skirt. In other words, it was fun, and she was, after all, only seventeen. The dress which drew everyone's breath was the one which she was to wear when she sang. It was floor length green silk, the color of her eyes. Augusta knew how to show her daughter off so well; and when Ruth saw herself in it for the fitting, she said that it was the first time in her life she felt like a woman, not a girl. Quite possibly, in this gorgeous dress she also experienced a mass of conflicting emotions.

Ruth had an underlying shyness that not everyone perceived; but she had also been a fairly spoiled child, and then, subsequently, a hardened young woman who was taught to suppress all her feelings. A dynamic cocktail of behaviors which had been impressed on her at a very young age. It's completely understandable that as she matured, she wasn't certain which way to lean. Who should influence her the most? All the values her parents had instilled in her existed, but the other firmer forces in the camp had made her realize that the only way to win was to be merciless. A deadly combination indeed, and one that would hound her throughout her life.

Opening night of the Show was a resounding success. Ruth's description was that the show was "Wonderful!" "It was like I was dreaming, and I turned up in Paradise." Each night was as successful as the first. "We had something of everything," said Ruth. "We opened with the two couples doing some sets of German dancing, the men wearing lederhosen and the women in dirndls. "The comedy routines were really funny, sometimes bordering on the burlesque, sometimes featuring humorous German songs, with people on the stage dancing and bumping into each other in risqué ways, with eyes rolling and the girls bending over to show their petticoats. Then between the laughing skits we had some serious ones," Ruth continued.

"The elderly violinist brought everyone to tears as he played a section from Violin Concerto No.1 in G minor by Max Bruch, the Prussian composer. Then later, he played Vivaldi's 'Winter,' taking everyone back to the time ten months before when they had arrived in Denmark in the bitter cold, tears of hopelessness pouring down their faces, not knowing a thing about their futures.

Ruth's first appearance on stage was at the very beginning when she played the piano for the comedic parodies. She was half-hidden from the audience as she, and Freidrich on his accordion, accompanied the players as they performed their antics. From that position on the stage it was impossible to see how many people were in the audience, but someone had whispered to her that the Hall was full! She was happy that Gertrude seemed to be enjoying the roles she had been given, and in that moment was proud that both she and her sister had achieved the first part of their dream to perform. In the first half of the Show the lady Yodeling champion delighted everyone with several Alpen songs. She invited anyone who wished to sing along with her to join her on the stage, but she was so good that nobody dared.

When Margot whirled on stage to perform her ballet recital, Ruth was still half-hidden from the audience, but she was thrilled with Margot, who gave a stunning performance and received at the end a standing ovation. At half-way time, there was a short break, during which Ruth had to change into her long black velvet skirt and white lace blouse. It was her turn to play solo piano.

The piano had been moved into the center of the stage, so when she walked up to it, sat on the stool and turned to face the audience, she had an unobscured view of everyone sitting in the Assembly Hall. There were some bright lights shining from the back of the hall, presumably to illuminate her, so her vision was slightly impaired as she looked down for her Mutti and Papa, but as she swept her eyes along the rows of seats, she caught her breath and her heart fluttered uncontrollably. Right in the front row, in the middle, she saw four men in uniform. The Commander, the Captain and their two Lieutenants. It took a minute or two for her to catch her breath! She had a fleeting feeling that if she played badly she would be punished; having only expected the audience to consist of refugees. Then common sense kicked in and she realized they were only there to see the Show like everyone else. She stood and bowed, looking everywhere but the front row, and then she sat and played. Chopin, Mozart, Debussy, Brahms. She didn't remember which pieces. Her face was flushed with joy and her determination to be perfect ruled her head.

When her recital was over, she stood, bowed to the audience and exited the stage; and behind the curtain, out of sight, she ran straight to the bathroom and vomited her nervousness away! Fredrich and Thea had a well-worn skit which they had played for years, and they performed it next; then came another burlesque. Ruth said it was a bit like the movie 'Cabaret,' very uplifting and optimistic. It was a deliberate positioning in the show, because Ruth was to come next as the last act, and she was going to sing classic and patriotic songs.

She changed into her beautiful green silk dress, shook out her long red/chestnut wavy hair, and when the music cued she stepped courageously on to the stage. The microphone was front and center, right in front of the Commander and his colleagues. In the past several minutes, something had changed; Ruth didn't know exactly what, but she followed her intuition and after bowing to the audience in general, she looked directly at Commander

Andersson. He was applauding like everyone else, and smiling; but as he looked directly in Ruth's eyes she knew that her performance that night would be for him, and him alone.

Then she began to sing. It was an uplifting and stunning performance. Some songs were dedicated to Germany and some were eternal classics, like 'Ave Maria,' but none of the songs were intended to offend and infuriate because they were Internationally beloved. At the end of her performance, everyone broke into loud applause and stood as one. She looked directly at the Commander and bowed her head. When she raised it, his eyes were locked on hers, and she knew in that moment that her world had shifted!

For each of the four nights that the little cast performed, the Commander was sitting in the same seat in the front row, and each night Ruth gained a little more confidence. 'This was the most powerful man in all their lives,' she thought, 'and yet he looks at me with such warmth and longing.' When the four days were over, at the end of the performance, Ruth, Margot and the Yodeling champion woman each received a bouquet of flowers, and stood in front of the audience glowing and radiant with happiness.

The next day though, Ruth said she felt as if nothing good could ever happen again. It was a huge let-down. No more was she the center of attention in every sense of the word, but life in the school reverted quickly back to normal and she became again a refugee amongst many others, who were given nothing but tasks and chores. Ruth's thoughts about the Commander began to change. Having believed that he had gone each night only to see her, she decided her thoughts were completely foolish. He went to the Show because he had to, she told herself. Since refugees from over the entire area had been invited to come and see their performance, of course, the Commander had to be showing support for his school, there was no way he was only going to see Ruth. That germ of a thought held fast, but deep down in her heart she felt a little ache.

After a month passed, Gertrude was taken to a hospital in Odense where she gave birth to a little boy. She stayed in the hospital for a few days, and when she returned to the school there was no child. Nobody asked any questions; it was a closed book. One can only surmise that the Commander had known, but had not reported the massive breach of rules. There was no way Gertrude would have been whisked off to hospital and be absent from the school for several days without him knowing. Quite possibly he was protecting himself as well as the Captain, since the Danish authorities would have also found him responsible and sentenced them both to execution.

After the theft of Ruth's Riding Boots, when she had such a hard time communicating with the authorities, she decided she would try to learn Danish; so as the boxes of books came into the school as donations from around the world, she started to look for books on language. It took a long time to find one in German to Danish, but finally, one was donated. It was a dictionary so she could only try to learn single words, but she was determined, and she proceeded to teach herself. Writing down German words and then writing next to them the same word in Danish, she spent hours on the project, but it was very slow and quite unsatisfactory. Then, one day, she overheard a young boy speaking Danish to his mother. The mother replied to him in German, which alerted Ruth to the fact that they were bi-lingual. When she spoke to the mother, she discovered that she had lived on the Danish/German border, and that her family spoke both languages.

Ruth said to the woman, "Would you mind if I look after your little boy for two hours each day? I would like to learn Danish from him, and in return you will have two hours to read or follow your hobbies, would that be acceptable to you?" The mother was delighted! "Oh yes, thank you." she said, "This is Jochim, he is ten years old and a very good reader." Then crouching down to her son's level, she said, "Jochim, will you let the Fraulein read your books with you?" The little boy nodded in agreement, and his mother smiled. "This will be very good for him," she said. "I don't need extra time to paint or draw, Jochim does that with me, but when I am doing kitchen chores for the school every day, Jochim has to stay with other children locked up in a classroom. Now, I can get permission for him to be with you, and you can learn from each other."

It was a perfect arrangement, so every morning Ruth and Jochim would meet in the hobbies room and practice their Danish. Within a few weeks Ruth was learning so fast that she was able to act as an interpreter and help the refugees who needed to speak with the authorities. Mostly, this brought her into contact with the Captain or lower-ranking officials, but occasionally, the Commander was needed to settle an issue. Each case was different; sometimes it was a trivial matter and sometimes it was serious, such as a person needing to see a Doctor. At all times, someone's permission had to be given. The first time Ruth needed to see the Commander, he looked up in astonishment to see that she was the interpreter, and he spoke to her in German. "Guten Tag, Fraulein, yetz sie bin ein interpreter?" "Good day, Fraulein, you are an interpreter now?" "Ya, Herr Commandant," she replied, "I have been learning your language." He flashed her a look which could only be interpreted as one of admiration.

She was a little shy, a little flustered, but the back and forth went quite well with only a few mis-pronounced words on her part. At the end of the discussion, Ruth thanked the Commander for his help, and again their eyes locked. She was truly bewildered, and hurried out of the room with the woman she had been helping. The confusion in Ruth's heart and mind was genuine. Why did this man look at her in this way? She was determined to just go on as before. There was no way she wanted to end up in the same situation her sister had encountered. Gertrude was still a refugee in a refugee camp. Nothing had improved her life.

Well, to be fair, one thing that Gertrude had succeeded at was to put pressure on the Authorities to find their Grandmother. It was in early September that the Lindenau family was informed by the Red Cross that Anna Lindenau had been located at a camp in Northern Denmark. It was one of the new camps which had been constructed to hold thousands of refugees. Within a week of being informed of that fact, Ruth's parents were told that their entire family would be sent to the new camp. Everyone was elated that darling grandma Anna had been located, but they were all nervous about being moved again. All the goings-on and activities that Ruth and her family had begun to relate to, were to be changed. They asked if Anna could be brought to them, but the request was denied. Danish authorities were trying to close all the small holding centers and consolidate the refugees into the large camps now completed.

It was in October, almost a year after arriving in Denmark and very close to Ruth's eighteenth birthday, when she and her family were put with many other refugees on a train bound for Aalborg. An area on the coast of Denmark, where Sea planes were launched. The new camp was enormous; completely different from the schoolhouse in Odense. The trauma of being re-housed in an official Refugee Camp cannot be underestimated. At this place several thousand people were being detained. It was just like a small town, but entirely surrounded by barbed wire, and everyone had to wear a uniform, exactly like a prison uniform. It was a full body suit in black and white stripes, and it was, said Ruth, totally humiliating.

Ruth and her family were delighted to reunite with Anna, whose strength and courage still shone through. With so many people in the camp it was only the strong and courageous who survived, and in spite of her age, Anna was a survivor. She was shocked when she saw her family! Fritz looking so much older and downtrodden, with his trousers hanging off his hips; Augusta, her strong daughter, looking so gaunt and stressed with the responsibility of bringing up her grandchild, and the months of worry for the whole family over Gertrude; Gertrude and Ruth, looking as beautiful as ever, but very thin; and the little Magrid, pretty like her mother, but obviously lacking a healthy diet, with blotches and spots on her skin and her little legs like sticks. Anna worried endlessly for her family, because she knew how meagre the food rations were and how poor the medical treatment for all the hundreds of emaciated detainees in this massive camp.

The huge numbers had resulted in serious nutritional and medical problems. Many people died there, and there was no-one to mourn. Life and death, it seemed, was interchangeable. There was never enough food and never enough medicine. If the school in Odense had been bad, this new camp was ten times worse. Small groups of people frequently went into town, usually to have some kind of medical treatment, because proper care in the camp was non-existent, and they were always escorted by two people. Anna spent hours trying to figure out how she could help her family, then one day, she told Ruth, "An angel gave me an idea."

One woman Anna knew, named Helen, had been to see a dentist in the nearby town. Her lack of nutrition over the past years had been a factor in the ruination of her teeth, so she had to get several of them removed. When Anna sympathized with her, the woman told her it was almost worth it, because going into town she had seen so many shops with beautiful things in the windows. One shop she couldn't stop talking about. It was a Baker's shop and the woman had said to Anna, "Oh!

The smell coming from that shop was like paradise! All the beautiful brotchen, fresh from the oven, and the kucken, decorated with fruits and chocolate, and the croissants and buns! Oh, Anna, I haven't seen or smelt anything like that for years! It was heaven!"

Upon hearing about this, Anna made up her mind that she too would go to town; and she would also find a way to bring back to camp some of that bread! Anna only knew one thing. Survival. She soon contrived a plan to get into town by pricking her gums with a sharp object until they bled, then telling the authorities that she had severe dental problems. She did this several times, sometimes crying in pain, and soon she was taken into town to visit the first dentist available. Anyone leaving the camp was allowed to wear their civilian clothing, partly for their own safety, because at this stage, even though the war was over, German people were despised, and the average Dane was furious that their country was hosting all the refugees.

Anna dressed in her usual long, gathered skirt and blouse with a colorful, wide apron over the top. A classical German style. After their appointments, everyone had to meet together to be counted, before walking to the train station and returning to camp. The guards were usually quite relaxed by this time, probably enjoying their trip into town, so once the group of refugees had been accounted for, everyone taken care of, the group would begin to walk along the busy sidewalk towards the station. One of the shops they passed was the bakery, the one that Helen had told Anna about. The smell of fresh bread was intoxicating as they approached, and when they reached the open door, Anna dived into the shop and grabbed a loaf of bread from one of the display baskets. The shop was crowded, so nobody noticed Anna quickly tucking the loaf under her apron. She hurried out of the store and quickly joined her group. She was so fast that she didn't think anyone saw her disappear, and by the time she was outside the bread was sitting snugly in a large pocket she had stitched on the inside of her apron.

Back in the camp, Anna gathered the family around her and produced the fresh loaf. She told them how she managed to pull off the deed, and seeing the huge smiles on everyone's faces, she broke the loaf into evenly sized pieces. Handing them around, she swore this would not be the first and only time she brought bread for her family! That was the case; over the next two years, Anna brought many loaves home! Helen, the lady who had given Anna the idea in the first place was never forgotten. Until the day she died, Anna called Helen "My Angel."

CHAPTER TWENTY

Ruth thoroughly disliked the new camp. Having been quite a celebrity in the Odense school, she was now one of thousands. She was still practicing her Danish, but amongst so many people in Aalborg she was just another detainee. And the black and white striped body-suit was an insult added to the injury. One day, after being in the camp for almost a year, she was on cleaning duty. That meant she was cleaning the streets. She recalls the day vividly.

"I was very miserable," she said, "I was not using any energy, just sweeping the leaves back and forth with a large broom, feeling very sorry for myself. There were people walking about, all of them had jobs to do and I ignored them. Then, out of the corner of my eye I saw a large black car. I didn't look up, but I knew that it had stopped very close to where I was sweeping. I kept sweeping and moving along the street and the car moved slowly alongside me. In the end I became curious, so I glanced up very quickly." she said. "The car was official looking, so I continued sweeping, a little faster, and as I moved along the street the car kept up with me. Then I became really scared. I thought the authorities were checking up on my work. I came to a round-about in the road and the car stopped right in front of where I was going. I didn't know what to do. It was like the car was blocking me so I had to look up directly. When I did, the window came slowly down and I saw him! Commander Andersson! He looked straight at me with that same look; the look I had seen when I sang in Odense, and he lifted his hand to his forehead in a kind of salute. Then the car drove off." Suddenly, for no logical reason,

Ruth's spirits lifted. The relief at not being punished was intense. The person who had lived in her heart for almost a year was there in Aalborg. She hoped, albeit a faint and illogical hope, that at last she could find a way to be saved.

Ruth's studies of Danish intensified. She was now able to find many people in this huge camp who could speak the Danish language, and she studied with all her might. Before too long she was fluent enough to apply for jobs in the camp. In the center of the camp there was a 'Town Center' of sorts, where all the administrative business was done. There was a small First Aid office which two Nurses ran, a schoolroom where children up to the age of fifteen were taught, and clerical offices from which Adult Occupation was administered. Everyone who was capable had to work. Everything from kitchen duties, road sweeping, painting buildings, garbage collecting, internal mail delivery, home repairs and child minding.

There was also a building for the Administrators. This was the largest building because it housed offices for the Danish Military and rooms for the guards, which included a dining room, bathroom and showers, sleeping accommodations and a security room for weaponry. Overseers of the camp had a store where they could buy personal items, and a recreation room where they could relax between duties. In this building was an office where refugees could go to air their grievances, get permission for medical attention or discuss issues connected to their appointed jobs around the camp. In this office there was a notice board which posted jobs needed around the camp; also, refugees looking for a particular type of job for which they qualified could post a note stating their capabilities. This is where Ruth went every day to look for an office clerk type of job. She was now almost nineteen and perfectly capable of office work. After a few days of looking and finding nothing posted for which she felt suited, she wrote her own post and pinned it to the board. "Office Clerk. Interpreter. Ruth Lindenau No. 961" was all she wrote. 961 was the little unit she shared with her family, and if anyone was interested to give her the work this is where they had to send a message. She posted her message in the morning and in the afternoon she received a notification. "Apply to Commander Andersson's office. Tomorrow. 9:00AM."

This was a miracle! At least, in Ruth's eyes it was. She barely slept that night and was awake in the morning 'with the lark.' She dressed in her striped clothing, and nervously waited until the time came when she had to walk to the Administration Offices. Upon arriving, she felt nervous, humiliated and expectant. A very complicated mixture of emotions. At 9:00 AM sharp the door to the Commander's office opened and her name was called. She stepped inside. The Commander was sitting behind his desk with an expression on his face which could only be interpreted as happiness or relief or a mixture of both. Ruth felt this in her innermost core. The man (which is what he was) was happy to see her. No longer a boss or a Commander, this is what he was. A man who cared about her. He hesitated when he tried to find words. His hands shook when he shuffled the papers on his desk. He was a captive to his emotions.

The incongruity was palpable. He was in charge of, literally, her life, and she was a refugee, a person who could be crushed underfoot. He was a married man of thirty nine, she was a girl of eighteen. The whole situation was intolerable. Yet, somehow, something was so powerful that fate had brought them together again. Ruth was never under an illusion that she had power. She always knew that she was the weaker person who had no choice but to go with the flow, but she couldn't deny that she had feelings for this man. She sat silently waiting for the Commander to speak. The first thing he did was to hire her on the spot! "Fraulein Lindenau," he said, "I would like you to work for me, be my assistant, help me with translations." He already knew that she was a talented and dedicated person. That she had studied to learn Danish and succeeded, and that she was the most fascinating person he'd ever known in his life. Of course the problem was that he was married and that he had an enormous responsibility; apart from the fact that fraternizing with the enemy was a cause for the death penalty.

Ruth cannot recall saying a word. She only remembers feeling shocked but also excited. The Commander rose from his chair and walked around his desk to where Ruth was sitting. He walked behind her, and putting his hands on Ruth's shoulders he gently said in the best German he could muster, "Fraulein Lindenau, I am guilty of thinking about you. Since the very first time I saw you in Odense I was captivated. Then I saw you singing and playing the piano so beautifully, and you completely filled my heart." Ruth turned to look up to him and her green eyes filled with tears. "For two years," the Commander went on, "you have been constantly on my mind, and when you left with your family to come here, I knew I had to follow you. I needed to know that you are well. I had to know that no harm had come to you." His own eyes teared up at that point, as he looked down at her, and Ruth knew then, without any doubt at all, that this man truly cared for her. They were both silent for several minutes, just letting the truth sink in, and then he continued. "I cannot do a lot for you in this situation, but if you work for me I can see you every day, and I will do everything in my power to keep you safe and well. If you need medication I can get it for you, and extra food for you and your family." Ruth nodded her head in agreement, as a feeling of sheer relief swept over her, and he squeezed her shoulders gently and bent down to kiss the top of her head. Then he returned to his seat, and became all business. "When you work for me," he said, "you can wear your civilian clothing, and you can eat lunch every day in the dining room here." "Yes, yes, thank you Mein Herr," said Ruth, suddenly finding her voice, "thank you for trusting me to work for you. I won't let you down."

Ruth's family were all delighted when she told them about her new job, minus the more personal information. Things in the camp were not improving, with supplies constantly running out, and inadequate medical help. The refugees had brought many diseases with them and resources to aid so many people were stretched to the limit. Contrary to the expectation of the Danish authorities, the British occupation force had decided that until Germany was stabilized the refugees must remain in Denmark, so it began to look like an indefinite period of time before anyone could go home.

Working every day in the office of the camp Commander was a bittersweet memory for Ruth. She began her job on September 1st in 1946. The war was already over, yet there was no sign of a notice of repatriation. Whilst she knew that he cared deeply about her, and she about him, the facts of post-war tragedies now came over her desk every day. In 1945 alone, the year the war ended, more than 13,000 people died in the camps of Denmark, and that included more than 7,000 children under the age of five.

The worst fact she had to deal with emotionally, was connected to the removal of land mines. In order to protect Denmark from being invaded by the Russian Army, German soldiers had buried what was estimated to be two million land mines all along Denmark's coastal western border. When Germany capitulated, this mass of deadly munitions had to be removed, and the British military who controlled the area made the decision that these prisoners should be deployed, and the Danish did not resist the order. Rather, they saw it as a way to punish the Germans for the war, so they ordered that all able-bodied men and boys should be given the dangerous task to remove the mines. German soldiers who had experience in neutralizing mines were put in charge of the mission. In fact, the decision violated the Geneva Convention, which prohibited anyone from giving prisoners any kind of dangerous work.

Nevertheless, the British military selected people, mostly German soldiers, many of them teenagers with no experience, who had been drafted into the German army in the final months of the war. They came from different camps, and were transported to a prison camp in Southern Jutland where they were given a three day course which taught them how to deactivate the land mines. In all, about 2,000 prisoners were sent to complete the task. Stories came back to Ruth's office that hundreds of men and boys were blowing themselves up, having been given nothing more than a broomstick to poke about in the sand to look for the lethal armaments. Young boys were seen crawling along on their bellies in the sand and dirt, and uncovering mines with their bare hands.

It was recorded that over 1,000, about half of these men, died as a result of this exercise, and many were crippled and permanently maimed. In later years a movie was made about the whole episode. Dead bodies were stored in cellars and warehouses, left unburied, left until negotiations on aid between the Danish and German authorities was resolved. The Danish wanted the liberation of about 4,000 Danish prisoners, many of them policemen, who had been captured by the Germans and put into concentration camps in Germany, including the one near where Ruth had lived, in Stutthof. The Danish Secretary of State, Nils Svenningsen, was adamant that nothing would happen until the prisoners were released, and the Germans said they would only release the prisoners if they were told to take an active part in defeating the Danish resistance. It was a stalemate which went on for months.

Ruth was working for Commander Andersson for almost exactly a year. He did as he had promised, and looked out for her well-being all the time she was in the camp. The feelings between them were kept well hidden. One slip, one hand holding, one stolen kiss, if observed, would have resulted in instant execution – probably for them both. The only time they were able to consummate their love for one another was on one occasion when Andersson had to make a trip to Copenhagen. He took Ruth along as his assistant and in the bustling city, with Ruth in her civilian clothes and he in his uniform, speaking only Danish, they passed off simply as husband and wife. Ruth told me that she will never forget the two nights they spent together. "He was", she said, "the love of her life." Certainly, he was her first love.

The trip to Copenhagen was, in fact, another bittersweet memory. Ruth explained, "He was at a meeting connected to discussions about repatriation. Many Danish camp administrators were there. Each being given information about when their own camp should begin to close down." On the way back to Aalborg on the train, Andersson told her about their own camp closure. It was to begin in July and be all finished by September that year. Ruth was both happy and profoundly sad. She was by now very much in love with the man who was going to secure her freedom to leave the country and go home to Germany. The situation was hopeless and they both knew it. Ruth remembers his words to her on the train. "Don't worry darling, I will write a letter for you to carry on the train. It will be a testament to your good character, and how you worked for me."

Over the next weeks, train-loads of refugees were packed into carriages and sent home to Germany, and the camp at Aalborg slowly began to shut down. Every refugee was given Forty Marks, which was provided to help them make a fresh start. A huge concern for Ruth was that most refugees were being returned to their original homes, but in her work with the Commander, she had read that the whole area around Danzig, including Tiegenort, was now Russian occupied. Clearly, to go back there would be intolerable. Ruth voiced her fears to the Commander, and he immediately understood the terrible dilemma, so he pulled some strings and arranged for her that she and her family would go to Freudenstadt in Southern Germany; to the French Zone of the country. "I was a bit worried about going to that region as well," Ruth said, "The Germans in the Black Forest area, the Bavarians, were notoriously known to intensely dislike people from Prussia; they considered the Prussian people to be overbearing war-mongers, but when I told my parents they were very relieved. They were much more afraid of the Russians," she recalled, "but they were also concerned when I told them I would be following them later. I wanted to stay until the bitter end." Ruth said. "And he, the Commander, needed me more and more to help with the translating, so I promised to stay. And the truth is, I dreaded the thought of leaving him."

When it was time for her family to leave, it was a very tearful goodbye. They had all been through so many separations over the years, and now, again, just as the time had come for them to begin to live their lives over, they had the fear that Ruth might not make it back to join them. Their fears were not unfounded. As the weeks went by Ruth was becoming more and more terrified at the thought of travelling alone on the long train journey. Stories of how the Germans were being treated as they went home by train abounded. At every Railroad stop, people actually waited there to hurl insults at the refugees and harm anyone they could get their hands on. Women were dragged off the trains, raped and left for dead. Nobody cared.

When it came for her turn to go, Andersson handed her the letter and the forty Marks which everyone was given to help them get started. He also gave her extra Marks in a little pouch which she hid in her clothing, and a bag of food for the journey. Sausage, bread, cheese. He gave her a Danish-style canvas hat, like a large cap, which he entreated her to wear at all times. She bundled her red waves into the hat, and with the jacket and floppy pants she wore she could have passed as a boy. The whole experience was overwhelming. He was profoundly sad. Ruth could see that in his eyes; and she was crying. That same day he was supposed to return to Copenhagen and attempt to pick up the tatters of his former life. They clung together in silence for a long while, knowing she had to leave for the station, and as she broke away he said, "Mein Schatz, sei in Sicherheit. Sag mir, wo du bist, wenn du nach Deutschland kommst. Ich komme, um dich zu finden." "My darling be safe. Tell me where you are when you get to Germany. I am coming to find you."

The trip to Germany was unforgettable. Ruth recalls hiding in corners on the train. Every time it stopped she hid under the seats. On the second day, she saw a man being pulled off the train when it had stopped to pick up other passengers. It wasn't hard to spot the refugees; they were terribly thin and sick-looking. The poor man had gone to look out of the open train door and to get some fresh air, when a gang of thugs spotted him, pulled him off the train and beat him mercilessly, then leaving him for dead on the platform. The fact that they were all wielding heavy sticks was a sure sign that they were lying in wait for the train to stop. Every time people walked past the carriage Ruth shrunk as far as she could into the corner. Always she did the same thing, so she was constantly on the look-out for people and could never relax. Only twice was she obliged to show her papers and both times they were accepted; she was certain the Commander's letter helped with her safe passage. She had only one thought which played over and over in her mind. 'Er kommt um mich zu finden' 'He is coming to find me.' When there was no food left in her little supply, that thought sustained her; when aggressive men with sticks came banging on the carriage windows, the thought sustained her. 'He is coming to find me.' It was a four day journey and each day she tried to make herself invisible, and eventually, they arrived in Freudenstadt.

CHAPTER TWENTY ONE

Ruth walked out of the train station onto Dietersweiler Strasse, at mid-day on September 18th, 1947. She was clutching one small leather bag containing her few clothes and toiletries, and with the strap held tightly across her body, she carried a cloth bag, holding her precious repatriation papers, some sheet music and the pouch of Deutschmarks. The beautiful Autumn morning could not have been more welcoming. The warm air smelled of pine and fresh baked bread, and the sharp sunlight intensified the colors, bringing all the beautiful Alpen-style buildings, and window-boxes overflowing with geraniums into sharp focus. The whole atmosphere made her feel like she was in Tiegenort. A feeling of sheer joy filled her heart as she looked around, and her throat swelled with emotion as she gazed at the scene; drinking in the architecture and the air gave her a strange sensation that finally she had come home.

She'd had no way to let her parents know when she would be arriving, but she had the address of the place where they now lived. Looking at the little town map she had picked up at the Bahnhof, she located the street and began to walk in that direction.

When she reached the house, one at the end of a row of neat little houses, she knocked on the door and waited. No sound came from within. She waited for a few minutes and knocked again. Still, no-one came. She didn't come this far to be disappointed, so she walked to the end of the street and turned left, hoping to see the back yards of the houses, and her heart leapt into her mouth! There was Augusta! Pinning laundry out on a clothes line slung across a tiny yard; and there was Magrid, hopping around and handing clothes pins to her Ooma! And sitting on an old metal framed chair by the back door was Fritz, contentedly puffing away on a pipe and enjoying the beautiful Autumn sunshine. It was a scene she had played over and over in her mind for years; this peaceful, happy scene in a German garden, and her heart spilled over with raw emotion.

Tears streaming down her face, she stumbled to a gate in the garden wall, and opening it up, with faltering steps she walked towards them. Words wouldn't come, she was choking with emotion. Augusta looked up in astonishment, thinking a stranger was entering the garden. Magrid stopped hopping about and Fritz lowered his pipe. They all stared at this stranger in amazement. Ruth lifted her arms to shoulder height and opened them wide, "Mutti," was all she could say, "Mutti, it's me." A howl escaped Augusta's lips and she ran to Ruth; her own arms open wide. They hugged in an embrace which would seem to never end. Then Fritz and little Magrid joined the group and they all hugged together, laughing and crying in sheer delight.

Finally, when the joyous noises abated, Augusta wiped her eyes on her apron saying, "Ruthchen, mein schatz, Ich habe dich nicht erkannt!" "Ruth, sweetheart, I didn't recognize you!" Ruth pulled off the canvas cap and shook down her red wavy hair; there was no mistaking her! Augusta had her darling daughter back where she belonged. Later that day, after a hot bath and some good German sausage and bread in her stomach, Ruth was able to tell her parents what she had learned just before the camp in Aalborg had closed. Some information was probably imprecise, but she knew for certain that the Russians, Americans, French and British had divided Germany into four regions for which they were now responsible. The area in which they now lived was French. The area in Prussia from which they came, plus all land as far as North Berlin, was Russian held, and the British and Americans had responsibility from Southern Berlin to Stuttgart. The Deutschmark was only exchangeable in Germany; and everyone who had legs and arms, hands and feet, was expected to help re-build this country, which had been bombed and torn asunder.

That evening, Gertrude returned home from her job, already assigned. She and numerous other young people had been taken to bombed areas and simply told to pile up the bricks. When Ruth asked Gertrude if that was the only work available, her sister said, "No. If you want to work on the land you can also do that. The choices are very limited at the moment. You can either help to provide food for the people or you can clear away bricks and stones."

Once in Freudenstadt, Ruth had to register and be put on record as a worker, so she spent a couple of days deciding what to do. She discussed the matter with her mother, and Augusta seemed to know exactly what would suit her daughter best. "Ruthchen," she said gently, "in Tiegenort you loved the nature. You loved to ride horseback and to walk in the countryside. Don't you think it would make you happier if you could work with plants and animals?" Ruth pondered her mother's advice. She remembered all the happy times in Tiegenort, but always skimming past the happy thoughts in her memory there were the thoughts of Munster Walde, where she and all the other girls were forced to dig up turnips and potatoes in freezing cold temperatures. Nevertheless, when her mother reminded her that the treatment here would not be the same, it gave her pause for thought.

'Yes,' she thought, 'if I can work on a nice farm in the Black Forest, look after the sheep, feeding the pigs and milking the cows, help make cheese and butter, be around the animals, I would be happier than choking on cement and brick dust in the city.' So her decision was made.

After registering and applying to the authorities, the last decision was made for her, and that was where she would go. It was to a Dairy Farm, sixty five kilometers from Freudenstadt. She packed her paltry few items in her leather bag, and then she sat down to do the one thing she had promised the Commander. Taking a sheet of paper and a pen, her hand shaking, she wrote:

My darling,

I arrived safely in Freudenstadt, thanks to your testimonial letter! I will soon be going to work in Pforzheim on a farm. If you can come, please send your letter to this safe address:

Fritz Lindenau, Freudenstadt,

Lossburgerstrasse 3, Deutschland.

My family will send your letter on to me.

I miss you so much. I love you so much. Please come.

Ruth

She kissed the letter, folded it, inserted it into an envelope and addressed it to the address he had given her. Then, telling Augusta she had a letter to post, she walked to the nearest Post Office. She knew it might take a while for the letter to arrive in Copenhagen, so she had no high expectations that she would hear back from him soon. But she had no doubt at all that she would hear back.

Once again, Ruth was leaving her family, but this time it was to a place much closer than before and there were no restrictions on either side. Whenever they wanted, her parents could go to visit her and whenever she had time off she could go to visit them. Therefore, when they said their goodbyes it was with a positive attitude and with hope in their hearts.

When Ruth arrived in Pforzheim, she was surprised to be met by a nice-looking man the moment she alighted from the train. He was blond haired and about thirty nine or forty years old. He didn't look like a man who worked on the land. Rather slim and not muscular and ruddy featured, he had more the look of a business man. In later years when she looked back, Ruth said he looked a lot like Robert Redford. "Fraulein Lindenau?" he enquired, and Ruth nodded. "Ja, Sir, ich bin sie." "Yes, sir, I am she." "Bitte, folgen Sie mir." "Please, follow me." He said, and reaching for her bag he took it and indicated towards a horse and buggy. They walked to the buggy and he helped Ruth into the seat in the front, next to where he sat. He wasn't a friendly person, yet he wasn't unfriendly either. Ruth had learned over the years to save her judgement about people until they began to show their true colors, and this was a classic example of a person she couldn't instantly read. She was now twenty, but oh! How much older she was in experiencing human nature.

When they reached a sizeable farm, about five kilometers away from the Bahnhof, the man drew his horse into a stable yard. He stopped the horse and then turned to Ruth. "I am Lukas Baumann. This farm was left to me by my parents, who both died in the War. I have a profession, but I need someone to take care of the business of this farm. I saw your qualifications and I think you will be able to keep the finances straight here. We are a Dairy Farm. I have people here who take care of the animals; we produce milk, cream, eggs and cheese. Every week we supply these products to purchasers, and I need someone who will make every effort to record each gallon of milk, each kilo of cheese and each pint of cream that leaves my farm. Fraulein Lindenau, can you do that?"

Ruth looked at him with confidence in her eyes. "Ja, mein Herr, Sie brauchen sich keine Sorgen zu machen." "Yes, sir, you have no need to worry." "You need to know, Fraulein, that we in Southern Germany do not trust anyone from the North. That includes me. I will be watching every move you make. Having officially employed you I have to, by law, give you work. I would have preferred hiring someone from here, but I had no choice." Ruth was not expecting this unashamed admission, thinking the feelings of Bavarians would be covert rather than totally blatant. She opened her eyes wide in surprise and looked Lukas Baumann directly in the face; in return she received a cold, hard countenance. "I will do the best I can do for you." She said aloofly, and turning her back on him, she jumped out of the cart and walked away.

Life on the farm was not so bad. Mostly, Ruth took care of the paperwork. The owner, Lukas, was away in Stuttgart every week at his Bank, and he only came home on weekends. He would arrive late on a Friday evening, and early on a Saturday morning he would send for Ruth to meet him in his office, which was in a small building across a concrete yard alongside the barns and milking stalls. Inside the office was a small bunk-bed, two chairs and a desk. Lukas told her that sometimes he would sleep in the bunk-bed when one or more of the cows were in calf. If they were having a difficult time, he could be easily woken up by the dairy-man and then he'd go to help with the birthing.

Every week, Ruth would go over all the items which had been sold on the farm, and gave him papers which had recorded the workings of the week. Almost always, unless there was a minor discrepancy, everything looked good, and he began to trust Ruth's business abilities. Not only that, he began to appreciate Ruth's charms. She had a modest approach toward him which he found fascinating. What he didn't know, was that all Ruth could think about, day after day, was her love for Commander Andersson in Denmark, and when he would write to her. Praying he would write to her.

Perhaps her very detachment toward Lukas played a part in his continuing interest, 'The Lure of the Chase', as it were, because as the weeks went by, Ruth could tell by his very attitude that he was becoming attracted to her. His moods, on the other hand, were un-nerving. Sometimes he seemed like a warm breeze of gentle air, and at other times he was like an icy blast of wind off the Alps! She decided to always remain steady and not respond. She had learned how to react to many different types of people over the years, so she behaved in a perfectly polite and friendly way toward him. Businesslike, but impartial. There was one person only, constantly on her mind, and it wasn't Lucas Baumann.

Weeks turned into months, and Ruth continued to work on the farm. Her parents came to visit her, and told her that Gertrude had fallen in love with a French Soldier and gone to live with him in France, leaving little Magrid to be brought up by her parents. Ruth wasn't surprised. Her sister was always self-involved and she felt that Magrid would be much better off with Augusta and Fritz. When she asked her parents if they had brought any letters for her, the answer, to her enormous disappointment, was no.

One weekend, Lukas came home, and his usual Saturday morning assignment was summoned. Ruth went to his office and she sensed that his mood had changed. For months now, she had made sure that all the finances of the farm were above board, and she had always provided paperwork to prove it. As a banker, Lukas knew and appreciated what Ruth had been doing, but instead of loving (or at least, liking) her for it, his bias about Germans from the North, especially Prussians, made him loathe her. At the same time he was madly attracted to her.

He met her in his office that weekend and Ruth sensed immediately a change in the atmosphere. She knew full-well by now that he was becoming attracted to her, she had learned well the signs; but she wasn't at all interested. There was only one man she loved, and she was waiting for him. Lukas listened to all her news about the farm's incomings and outgoings, but while she was talking he was fidgeting, and she could tell that something else was on his mind. Then quite suddenly he moved around his desk and pointed his finger at Ruth, shaking with anger. "You! You are a traitor!" He yelled. Ruth was nonplussed! What on earth was he talking about? "You killed my parents." He said, with agony in his voice, "You killed them!" And he slumped to the floor.

What could she say? A lifetime of killing and sorrow. Her head spun with stories of horror. She knew her history, knew full well how the Prussians were not liked, but for him to blame her, she just wasn't prepared for that. Maybe his parents were Jews, she didn't know. "What are you talking about?" She shouted, then moved toward him slowly, her head bowed, giving herself time to consider what she could say; thinking she could get him to explain. He looked up at her angrily, with tears in his eyes. He was shaking with emotion when she came closer, and he struggled to his feet, facing her. "What do you mean?" Ruth asked quietly, "Why do you say such a thing?" "You bloody well know!" He spat back at her. "You people have never been trusted by us Bavarians; you have never been liked".

He took her by the shoulders and shook her, pushing her onto the bunk-bed. Pinning her down with one heavy hand he ripped off her blouse, and pulled up her skirt with the other. Then he lay on top of her and pushed himself into her. He thought he was making love she knew she was being raped. It was like a catharsis; for him, that is. His head had been full of loathing, but was slowly being replaced by a strong, almost obsessive attraction to her. He wanted to love her and punish her at the same time. He was completely out of his mind; he was ashamed and confused with his own feelings! Ruth was an innocent child when the horrors of their War were being played out; and she too, since thirteen years old, had suffered greatly at the hands of her own countrymen.

After the attack, he held Ruth and almost frantically hugged her tight and kissed her over and over, saying he was sorry. He tried to explain to her what was in his head, and then he told her what was in his heart. Ruth was completely in shock, but the tough training she had undergone in Munster Walde had made her resiliant. After his apologetic diatribe, and then his declaration of love, she lay there on the bunk bed, staring at the ceiling. "I am trying to understand what you say," she said quietly, with no emotion in her voice, "but I don't think I should be the brunt of all your mixed feelings. I told you I would work for you and be an honest and faithful employee. That I have done." With that, she got off the bed and walked out of the office.

Lukas was not in a position to fire her. Indeed, he still hoped to salvage the disastrous situation he had created. The weeks went by as before. Ruth looked after the books and did her job well and he came home, as always, on Friday nights. The only difference now though, was that he was perfectly polite and well-behaved with Ruth. It was clear to her that he was trying to win her over. Then one day, one morning, Ruth thought she was becoming ill. She couldn't even look at her breakfast, instead, she had to run to the bathroom and vomit. She fully understood in a couple of days that she was suffering from the exact same thing her sister Gertrude had suffered from in Odense. Yes, she was pregnant! The first thing she did, when Lukas came back on the following weekend, was to ask him if her parents could come to visit. He was now a much altered person in her presence. Someone who wanted nothing more than to make her happy. "Of course they can come to see you, Ruth. And ask them to come on a weekend while I am here, I would like very much to meet them." He murmured, always seeking her approval. So, in a few weeks, (it took time for mail to be exchanged), Augusta and Fritz came to the farm with Magrid.

Ruth had to take her mother aside. She didn't want to tell her story with Magrid in the same room, so she asked her father to take Magrid to go and look at the horses in the barn. When she and her mother were alone together, Ruth turned to Augusta and they looked in each other's eyes. "Ruthchen," said Augusta gently, "I know. You are having a baby." Ruth's green eyes filled with tears. This mother with whom she had been through so much, knew her daughter better than she knew herself. Augusta reached for Ruth's hand, and together they walked outside into the farm; and while walking through the fields of cattle and sheep, Ruth told her mother everything.

When they returned to the house, Augusta told Ruth that her father needed to know. Ruth took Magrid to see the ducks in a nearby pond, while Augusta told her husband. They had both met Lukas the day before, as he had requested. They had found him charming, intelligent and obviously delighted with their daughter, who he had praised to the high heavens. For Augusta and Fritz there was an easy solution. Ruth should marry him.

Chapter Twenty Two

When Magrid was tucked up in bed that night, Ruth and her parents had a serious discussion. Ruth made it clear that she didn't love Lukas, but she went no further than that. She didn't tell her parents that she loved the Commander of the prison camp where they had lived and almost died. How could she tell them that, when she hadn't heard a word from him in over a year? She still hoped, but was already telling herself it was a hopeless dream. The conversation went back and forth until she was exhausted. And then, by sheer chance, Lukas was knocking on the door, wanting to say goodbye before he left next morning for the Bank in Stuttgart.

He entered a room of intense atmosphere, and in a minute or two, quite unlike him, Fritz was the first one to speak. "You don't know this," he said unsteadily, "but my daughter is pregnant with your child." Lukas, who Ruth was expecting to deny everything, opened his eyes in amazement and ran to Ruth, hugging her, laughing and crying, full of joy. "This is wonderful news!" he cried, "So we can now get married!" Ruth, her eyes wide in amazement, was shocked beyond belief. She looked at her parents who were both smiling and nodding their heads in agreement. "Ja, Ruthchen, du weisst, das ist das Beste." Said Augusta. "Yes, Ruth, you know that is for the best." Fritz walked over to Lukas and shook his hand in both of his. "I hope you will make my daughter happy, Herr Baumann." he said, "We are pleased to welcome you into our family." Ruth looked at her parents; eyes and mouth open wide, looking beseechingly from one to another. Not wanting what was being forced upon her, but yet, not having a better alternative. It would seem that the decision had been made; it was as if she wasn't even in the room. In less than a month, Ruth married Lukas very quietly in a Civil ceremony in Freudenstadt; with just her parents in attendance.

Ruth didn't talk too much about the next two years of her life. The happiest spot on her horizon was the birth of her only child, her beautiful daughter, Barbara. She and Barbara lived on the farm, and their time during the week was, as Ruth recalled, blissful. She adored and idolized her beautiful baby girl. Sometimes, she would leave her for an hour or two while Barbara slept, with one of the women who looked after the chickens on the farm, and she would saddle up one of the horses and ride into the countryside. But mostly, she lived and breathed with her daughter in her arms. Barbara was truly her miracle. Those days, for Ruth, were idyllic. She was married to a man who was twice her age, yet he was delighted with his daughter and kind and loving with Ruth. She still had intense feelings for the Commander, and knew she could never feel the same about Lukas, but he had provided her with a good home and the strongest sense of security she had felt since she was thirteen years old. She began to luxuriate in that feeling; in the sense that she now had a refuge. And she was determined to be a good and faithful wife.

At the beginning of her marriage, Lukas made every effort to make Ruth happy. He came home from the Bank every week, clearly excited to see her. During the weekends he would take her out and about into Pforzheim; buying her pretty things and trinkets in the shops; taking her for Kaffee und Kuchen in the local Konditorei. Showing her the beautiful areas around the town; taking her for hikes and picnics into the countryside. They grew closer together during that time, though both of them had a lifetime of agony to hide. So they skirted around it when they talked. She couldn't bring herself to talk of the years of pain and hurt she had experienced; and he, on the other hand, found it impossible to tell her how the Nazis had come to his home, banging on the door and demanding to see his two younger brothers, so they could be brought into the Hitler Youth in this insane War which was just beginning.

He was already away from home then, studying, and his two brothers were the only ones left at home. When his parents heard that the Nazis were coming, they told the boys to run! "Lauf!" Run! The boys ran, and the Soldiers were soon enough at the farm, demanding of his parents where the boys were. His mother told them all her boys were away studying in Stuttgart, but the soldiers had everyone's information so they knew she was lying. They grabbed his mother and yanked her head back by her hair. Then they cut her tongue out. "This is what you get for lying." They said, "And also this!" and they turned to her husband and shot him on the spot. Lukas had no idea what happened to his brothers. He just knew that the boys ran and had not been heard from since. The unbearable pain had undoubtedly affected him profoundly. He knew what had happened because some workers on the farm had witnessed the entire episode. Nazi soldiers were not at all bothered about showing what happened to people who defied them. It was a fine way to keep the population under control. Within six months, his mother died. She was found hanging in a barn on the farm with a rope around her neck, and Lukas never knew if it had been murder, or if she just couldn't face living anymore.

It was at least a year before Lukas was able to tell Ruth about his parents, around about the time Barbara was six months old. Having seen many terrible sights herself, and with the stoic side of her nature prevailing, perhaps Lukas felt she showed little sympathy, but within a short time of telling her, his attitude toward her shifted again. It was very subtle, and over a long period of time, but she felt strongly that his feelings for her were divided. He was just as loving and affectionate with Barbara, but with Ruth he became colder and sometimes openly hostile.

Then, one weekend, one Sunday, they had been on a picnic to a nearby Park. Just the three of them. Ruth, Lukas and Barbara. There was a lake with swans, and other people there having a good time. Lukas started to talk about how his brothers used to love this lake. How they would come with their model boats and ask him to steer them to the shore because his arms were longer. He was their big brother at University, studying to be a Financier, and they were very proud of him. Lukas sunk into a mood of despair. Nothing Ruth could do or say would change his mood. It became so intolerable that she began to dread Friday nights when he came home. Instead of being the easy-going man she had come to know. Now he would arrive on a Friday night and begin drinking, his mood morose. Ruth had compassion for him, and she tried hard to steer his mind in a more positive direction, but the alcohol failed to help. He drank more and more, and then he became violent.

Barbara was about a year old when Ruth decided she had taken enough. Her husband was two people. One who hated her and one who loved her. And the two parts were constantly quarreling in his head. It was as though he needed her to bring back his parents. One Sunday night, before he left the farm, he came to their bed and started to berate her. His entreaties were incoherent, but they amounted to the fact that he was blaming her again. For a war that started when she was twelve years old. When she tried to pacify him, to tell him he was being illogical, he grabbed a lamp from beside the bed and raised his hand to smash it down on her. Fortunately, Ruth was half his age agile, and she was sober. She leapt from the bed and ran to baby Barbara's room where she locked herself in and stayed for the night. When Lukas had sobered up in the early hours of the morning, he came and banged on the door, telling Ruth how sorry he was and to please forgive him. She ignored his entreaties. It had happened far too often to forgive.

The following day, when she knew that Lukas had left for Stuttgart, she packed up her few possessions, and all her daughter's belongings, and she asked one of the farm workers to take her to the Bahnhof. She was heading back to Freudenstadt and her parents. Once again, she was knocking at the door of her parents' home, and this time they heard her. Certainly, they were shocked to hear her story, and greatly angered that Lukas had treated their daughter in such a way, but they welcomed Ruth and Barbara with open arms, and promised to help her in any way they could.

Life in Freudenstadt was much easier. There were many new residents moving there when the war was over, but unless they were registered for work, mainly young people, nobody knew where they came from. Certainly, their accent was different, but not necessarily identified as of Prussian origin, so mostly people were accepted on face value. It was only because Ruth, as a young person, had been obliged to register for employment, which stated where she was born, that she was recognized by Lukas as a Prussian. Maybe because of that fact, or maybe because in these post war times it was easier, Ruth, with the help of her parents and, it should be said, total cooperation from Lukas, she was able to walk into the Town Hall in Freudenstadt and obtain a divorce. Lukas signed a document that he would provide for his daughter until she was eighteen, and he faithfully did so.

One of the possessions Ruth had brought home with her to Freudenstadt, was a knitting machine. Lukas had asked her what she would like as a wedding present, and that was her choice, so he bought her one. She had spent hours during her pregnancy knitting little outfits for her new baby and then had graduated to making sweaters and scarves for Lukas, and all kinds of items for herself and Barbara. She loved inventing patterns and creating different things, and one day after she and Barbara had been in Freudenstadt for a month or two, Fritz came home very excited. He had spotted on one of the main streets in the town that there was a store space for rent.

Fritz, being a qualified Tailor, had seen an opportunity to earn money for the family. Fritz was a perfectionist. His suits and jackets were second to none, and he knew that with a store where people could come and see his work and order clothing, he could make a good living. He told Augusta and Ruth about his plan and immediately Ruth said she could go with him and make knitted items to sell in the store. It was an idea they couldn't resist. In idea made in heaven. And it worked! In less than two weeks Ruth had installed her knitting machine in the window of the store, Fritz had found an old dressmakers dummy, a desk and a couple of chairs, some hanging racks and some shelving, and they were ready to open for business. Ruth had made a lot of items whilst living in Pforzheim, many of which her family would never use, so she stacked the shelves in the store with them. Mostly scarves, gloves and hats, but a couple of sweaters too. Augusta also had some beautiful shawls which she had made and packed away, surplus to requirements, so they also went into town to the store. All they needed now was a long table for the workroom, where Fritz could measure out bolts of cloth, also needed for suiting; so selling the knitted items was critical in order that they could invest in the table and the fabrics.

Fortunately, winter was around the corner, and the colorful gloves, scarves and hats were soon snapped up by the locals, if not for themselves, as Christmas gifts. And as winter closed in, the beautiful shawls, too, were in demand. Fritz was delighted, as he was soon able to buy the all-important items for his tailoring business. Both Augusta and Ruth were now kept busy doing the thing they loved. The war was over and people still didn't have a lot of money to spend, but for a special Holiday like 'Weinachten', 'Christmas,' it was when they were willing to dig a little deeper into their pockets. When Ruth went to the store, she brought Barbara in a bassinette, wrapped up in a warm blanket, and she placed her baby next to her while she sat in the window and knitted on her machine. As time went by, ladies in the town wanted to learn how to knit, having seen Ruth turn out so many lovely items, so before long Ruth gave classes on how to work the machine. On those days, when she was teaching, Augusta took care of Barbara, and little Magrid, who was now seven or eight, helped her Ooma take care of her baby cousin.

By this time, Fritz had built up a very nice Tailoring business as well. His work was immaculate, and since exactness and perfection ran in the blood of most Germans, he soon had a loyal following of clients, who recommended him to all their friends. It would seem that now, the Lindenau family had about as much of their share of life's happiness and contentment as they could. But life? Fate? Karma? Has a strange and marvelous way of leading us all astray.

In the town of Freudenstadt lived a family called Raible. The senior Raible, Heinz, owned an abattoir, supplying meat of all kinds to the surrounding areas. His son, Karl, when he was old enough, ran the family Metzgerei, Butcher Store, in town, which happened to be a few stores more, down the same street as Fritz's Tailor and Knitting store. Every morning, Karl would walk to his store past Fritz's store, and sitting in the window, setting up her knitting machine, lo and behold! Her green eyes would meet his blue eyes most mornings and after a short eternity, Karl plucked up courage and stuck his head in the door of Fritz's store. He looked at Ruth. "Guten Morgen," he said "wie die Geschafte laufen?" "Good, morning, how's business?" "Good, thank you." Said Ruth, and with that he walked to the back of the store and the two men talked about business in general and introduced themselves to each other. Fritz then walked Karl towards Ruth and introduced his daughter, then, pointedly, he crouched down to the bassinette containing Barbara and introduced his grand-child. Karl was as calm as could be. He was a man not easily flustered. He bent down and chuckled little Barbara under her chin with his index finger. "What a little beauty," he said, "just like her mother."

As always, Ruth knew when she got 'the look.' The look that meant a man was more than just interested. Karl flashed her that look as he stood straight and walked towards the door. 'He is a fine young man,' thought Ruth, 'confident and polite. The kind of man who could be a good friend.' On most days after this, on his way to his store, Karl would open the door to Fritz's store and pop his head in. "Guten Morgen allerseits!" "Good morning, everyone!" He would shout out, if Ruth and Fritz were in the back of the store. "Don't worry, its only me, your friendly butcher." If Ruth happened to be in the window on her knitting machine, Karl would open the door quietly, then he would step close to her and say, "Guten Morgen, sweet Ruth, how are you today, and how is little Barbara? I've come to wish you both a shining day." Whenever he came, he always brought a smile to Ruth's lips and after a few weeks it got to the point that she would look forward to his visits.

Karl was never pushy, he seemed to have an innate sense that Ruth had been through a lot, and he wasn't about to drive her away. Some days, as the weeks went by, he would come at lunch time and bring his home-made wurst and bread. On those days, Fritz invited Karl to join them, and they would sit at the long table in companionable silence while they munched his kind offering, or in interesting, friendly conversation when the only food left was crumbs. Ruth's first impression was absolutely correct; Karl was becoming a good friend. Someone she and her father felt they had known far longer than they really had. For Karl wasn't afraid of speaking his mind, which gave them insight into his character, without having to poke and prod for information. For one thing, he had a marvelous sense of humor, an enormous asset, since in these times after the war people didn't find themselves laughing so much.

Karl also had a wonderful view on life. He was young and energetic enough to understand that a whole world was out there. That the Black Forest, albeit stunningly beautiful, was not the only place where one could live happily. He was extremely disillusioned with the terrible situation his country had created, and he wasn't proud. He absolutely wasn't proud. During the times he sat at the table with Fritz and Ruth, he told them about his dreams of maybe moving to another country to try and start again. He talked about South Africa, he talked about USA, he talked about Canada, Australia and New Zealand. This fact alone gave Ruth the confidence to allow their friendship to develop. She knew that Karl was not going to stop anything from following his dream, and that included Ruth.

CHAPTER TWENTY THREE

So, they eventually met one evening on a real date. They went to a rustic restaurant, listened to German music and danced. Karl was a real gentleman, he was enjoying his evening with Ruth, and he let her know it, but he let her lead the way. He already knew that 'no pressure,' was the only way to win her over. It was over two years, now, since Ruth had been in Germany, and still no word from Commander Andersson. She loved him still, those first love feelings never fade, but the circumstances had been surreal. Ruth felt she had matured beyond her years. A divorced woman with a child. Even if Andersson came to find her, how would he react when he saw she had a daughter? How would he react if he knew she had been married?

She decided to write to him again. Telling him everything about her time in Germany and begging him to reply. This, she did, and again she kissed the letter as she mailed it. In the meantime, she was a busy mother and daughter with a business in the town, and her life was beginning to feel fulfilled. She and Karl spent more and more time together. It was clear that he cared deeply for her, and he set her at ease with his kindness and wonderful sense of humor. She thought often that to find herself laughing and feeling happy was a new experience. Since her childhood these feelings had eluded her, and now, because of Karl and her daughter, she felt a sense of peace that she'd never felt before. The months went by, and no letter came, and slowly but surely her acute feelings of love for Commander Andersson decreased. When she went to bed at night, or if she sat down and began to think of him, the strong emotions returned immediately; but during the days, she was so busy that she would even feel a little guilty that she had not thought about him for several hours.

It was during this time that, once again, Ruth had to make a life-changing decision. Karl asked her one day if she would go with him for a hike in the forest. "Bring Barbara," he said, I have a strong canvas bag which I can sling over my shoulders and carry Barbara on my chest. It will be good for us. The fresh air and the nature." Ruth loved the idea. She enjoyed walking, as did almost all Germans, and she hadn't explored the local walking areas since arriving in Freudenstadt. They planned to pack a picnic and set out the following weekend.

A gorgeous April day! Fresh, clear and sparkling! Ruth said she would never forget the day. Karl met her and Barbara at Ruth's house, with a canvas bag, straps crossed over his shoulders, all ready and prepared with a warm blanket to snuggle Barbara into it. The little child tolerated being swaddled in the blanket and tucked safely into the bag. As she looked at her daughter, Ruth couldn't help thinking how comfortable she looked with Karl. No tears, no struggling to be with her mother; it made Ruth feel that they were a contented little unit. Augusta had made a meat pie for their picnic, obviously encouraging the couple; and she packed cheese, tomatoes, apples and bread for them, and napkins and a flask of wine. They set out with a sense of purpose, and walked for a couple of miles until they reached a wooded area next to a lake. Entering the pine woods gave Ruth a sensation of the time she had been with all the girls from Munster Walde. A shiver ran through her, and Karl noticed. "What happened?" He asked. "Oh, just a bad memory from my past," replied Ruth, and when Karl looked at her she had tears in her eyes. A stream was twinkling and bubbling next to them, and Karl stopped, crouched down next to a rock and patted it, signaling Ruth to sit down. He sat next to her, a sleeping Barbara, close to his chest. "Ruth," he said gently, "if you want to tell me, I'm here for you, but if you don't want to talk about it, I'm also here for you." And Ruth lay her head on his shoulder and wept. When there were no tears left to cry, Ruth told Karl a little about her experience at Munster Walde, but she couldn't bring herself to go into detail. She quickly moved her story to Odense, how she had met the Commander of the Danish camp, and then on to Aalborg, where she told him the Commander had moved there to be near her. She admitted to Karl about the love she had for this man, and that she was hoping he would come to find her as he had promised.

To her great surprise, Karl did not judge her. He simply held her tight. They sat for some time in this cocoon of vulnerable honesty, and then it was Karl's turn. "Ruth," he began, "you know I have told you I want to begin a new life, somewhere far away from here? Well, I need to tell you that I have just decided what I want to do. I'm going to live in America. I have discovered that the American Government is willing to take refugees from Germany who want to begin a new life, and that is exactly what I want to do. After all your torment Ruth. After everything you have been through, would you consider coming with me? I can offer you and Barbara a chance of a new beginning. Darling Ruth, I want to marry you." Ruth knew in her heart that this was what Karl wanted, but she needed to be honest with him. "Karl," she began, "you now know everything about my past life. You know I still have feelings for Commander Andersson, but I've almost lost hope he will come now. I've come to regard you as my best friend, and I am really very fond of you. If you can live with that, I will make you a promise here and now. If I become your wife, I will go with you to wherever you want to go, and I will never mention the past again."

Karl had tears in his eyes as he looked at her. "And I," he said, "will never, ever, let you and Barbara down."

They had their picnic by the stream, and hand in hand they walked back to Freudenstadt. Very little was said; they had a plan and they both knew that their real new life was just beginning. The next day Ruth sat her parents down and told them what Karl was about to do. He had already obtained papers, and had submitted them to the Embassy. In a few short weeks, he would be leaving for America, and he had to live there for one year before he could send for his wife and child. Augusta and Fritz had been through so much that they could only wish their daughter well. They liked and trusted Karl and knew that he would make their daughter and grand-daughter happy.

The pair were married in the Town Hall in Freudenstadt, and only Augusta and Fritz were present. Karl's parents were not happy at all about the union. He was very distressed that they were not at his wedding, and he begged them to give his wife and her child a chance. He managed to persuade them to let them live together in their home until he left for America. They were not delighted with the plan, but they agreed. Torn between their love for their son and their dislike of his future plans.

It wasn't easy for Ruth, but they moved immediately after the wedding into Karl's parent's home. It was a large and beautiful farmhouse, just outside of Freudenstadt. They were there for the few weeks before Karl left for America. He had wanted that badly, because he hoped very much that his parents could be brought around to accept his marriage. During that whole period of time life was very difficult for Ruth. Her in-laws were, to begin with, very upset that their son had chosen to marry a woman who had another man's child. At that time, this kind of relationship was deeply frowned upon; and on top of that, their son was moving to America, an action for which they both blamed Ruth. In fact, Karl had wanted to start over again, before he even met Ruth, but his parents both felt that he was trying to get away from their disapproving comments after his marriage. To be fair, in many parts of Europe at that time, tradition and standards were very important. Even though the war had thrown millions of people's lives into disruption, the traditionalist older generation were adamant about their views on what was 'proper.'

Karl desperately wanted to bring Ruth and Barbara into his parent's home in the hopes that they would become fond of Ruth and attached to her little girl, but it was not to be. They were determined to make everyone's life miserable, so after he left, unable to move the pendulum her way, Ruth moved back with her parents. It was exactly a year later that she received notification that she and Barbara were cleared to go and join Karl in America.

She said her goodbyes at home. She didn't want her parents to come to Munich, because she knew that leaving Freudenstadt would be an emotional time for everyone, and she didn't want Barbara to get frightened with everyone crying at the airport. She decided to tell Barbara they were going on an adventure to see Daddy, preferring to take the train to Munich, where they would board the plane which would take them to America. She had booked into a hotel in Munich because the flight was very early the next morning. She arrived in the late evening at the hotel and checked herself and Barbara in. They went up to their room and Ruth fed Barbara, unpacked her nightclothes, and they settled in for the night. Next morning, just as they were ready to leave, there was a knock at the door. A member of the hotel staff handed her a letter. "Sorry to bother you, madam," he said, "but the Butcher, Heinz Raible, from Freudenstadt, who supplies us with meat, delivered this letter which he said came for you from his home."

Ruth took the letter, assuming it was from her new in-laws for she and Karl to read together, hoping it was a letter to make peace with them, so thanking the person for bringing it to her, she put it straight into her bag. Taking the bus to the airport, Ruth was very nervous. She had never flown before, so she tried to allay her fears by talking to Barbara about their great adventure to go and find Daddy. Barbara was as good as gold, and played along, taking it all in stride as most children will. Getting through the airport and then going to wait for their flight, Ruth felt a flutter of excitement. They really were going to live in a new country; the rest of her life was about to begin. Karl had settled in New Jersey, and was working three jobs, in order to save as much as he could for their new home. In the mornings he delivered newspapers around the area in which he lived, during the days he was a butcher in a large grocery chain store. He had told her in his letters about the town he lived in, and how much he liked being there, so she was excited to see it herself.

As they boarded the plane and were shown to their seats, Ruth began to relax for the first time in two days. They were on their way! The plane started to taxi down the runway, and Ruth looked out of the window, wanting to say a silent goodbye to Germany and her family; a final look at the gorgeous countryside. They were taxiing past a lush, green field, and as the plane's wheels lifted from the ground, a rush of air disturbed a group of nesting larks. They flew upwards from their nests, straight into the clear blue sky, and as the plane rose higher, the larks kept pace. For several minutes they flew alongside Ruth's window, and then they disappeared.

Once they were airborne, Ruth remembered the letter in her bag and took it out to read it. As she looked at the Danish postmark and opened the envelope she gasped and struggled to breathe.

My Darling:

After you left I was ordered to attend an official tribunal. It was suspected that I gave favors to you and your family. On just a suspicion with little evidence I was found guilty and sent to prison.

I served four years. I am now divorced and I am coming to find you in the Black Forest. Nothing matters about your past. I understand. Please wait for me my darling.

Drews Andersson

THE END

Epilogue

Ruth arrived in America with Barbara and began a new life. She had promised Karl that she would never talk about her past again and she didn't; not for fifty years. Karl always knew that underneath her brave, and sometimes brash exterior, she had a kind, loyal and generous heart. Like her father, Fritz, she was a perfectionist, which could sometimes be a little intimidating for her family, especially her daughter, who tried always to reach the unattainable for her mother. Although Ruth certainly had the kind qualities of both her parents, the indoctrination she received at the hands of the Nazis had a lasting impression on her soul. Sometimes she was perceived as being hard, stubborn, or even callous, when in actual fact she was being self-protective. This is the skill she learned in Munster Walde; never let anyone 'get to you.'

There was always a fear in her innermost core that she would be exposed! That someone might discover she was really a frightened person inside, who was desperate to chip away the ugly exterior and show her family who she really was; but it was never to be. The influence of the brainwashing she experienced lasted until the very end. She could never relax enough to fully expose her true self. I also believe that as she aged she used her hard outer shell as a form of protection, since, the more she aged the more sentimental she became, and she was frightened by that weakness. In spite of that, everyone who loved her, somehow sensed her kind and softer side, and all admired her for her strength and fortitude.

I met Ruth when she was in her early seventies; she was still a handsome woman. Tall and arresting, with her green eyes and red hair still giving her a striking appearance, though her hair was now cut short. A friend, Penny Campbell, to whom I shall always be grateful, had told me she knew a lady who had an incredible tale to tell. As a biographer, I'd been told that many times, only to be disappointed; but after an initial three hour meeting with Ruth, when she opened up her heart to me, I knew that her story had to be told. I asked her why she needed to tell this story after so many years of keeping it a secret. She explained that she had made a promise to her husband Karl to never talk about it. Their new life in America would be a new beginning and the past would stay in the past. Karl, of course knew what she had told him before they married, but he only knew half her story. Over the years, as her daughter grew up and then her grand-son, they naturally asked her questions about her past and she mostly told them as little as possible and brushed them off with a comment like, "Oh, it's all in the past, I try to forget about it."

There was a newspaper article about her life, after she moved to Florida; but the story published barely scratched the surface of the experiences she had, and a great deal was left out altogether. After her husband died, she told me she had thought about one thing only, and that was to tell somebody everything about her experiences. She was still very reluctant to tell her daughter, Barbara, because she knew that over the years she had not been completely honest with her, and now she didn't want to face the consequences of her admissions.

I believe she trusted me for several reasons. I had already written a book about a couple living in America, who had become world famous in the 1950's. They had trusted me with their own life stories and a lot of confidential stories about famous people, which I kept private at their request. I spoke her language having lived in Stuttgart for some years, and I had loved every minute of it; so I believe Ruth knew that I liked and understood the German people. Some of my husband's and my closest friends were German and I told her, truthfully, that for my whole life I had thought I was, in another life, a German Jew. Perhaps crazy, but I truly believed it, until I got a DNA test and discovered I was wrong! In any event, Ruth could tell I had an open mind, and she was right.

I knew first hand, from stories I was told, what many German people suffered at the hands of their own people, and Ruth, without any doubt, was one of them. Her story warrants being told. It is one of courage and love. Of loyalty and commitment; and her family deserve, and need to know, all the nightmares she lived through which created the woman she became. She trusted me to know everything about her past, an honor I cherished. When we got together and talked, it was like receiving a flood of information, pouring out of her. She had kept her word and not told the whole story until I agreed to write it for her, and then the floodgates opened. She had held it all inside for so long that I could sense the relief as she talked. All kinds of documents, photos and letters were shown to me, which she had kept boxed up for all those years. Letters on dark paper, written with old typewriters and vague, faded lettering. Obviously genuine. I touched them, read them, and my soul was riveted. This woman had really been through hell and back.

After working on the book for close to a year, I was so emotionally committed to it that I felt I needed to go to Poland and visit Tiegenort, now called Tujsk. My husband, Ken, is always incredibly supportive of my writing, and he agreed we should go. On the way, we were going to visit my father in England, who was very sick and not expected to live. Without going into too much detail, upon arriving in Poland we were met by a charming man, who the staff at the hotel we were staying in, had arranged should meet us at the airport. He spoke good enough English for us to converse, and on the hour long trip to the hotel he gave us an amazing amount of information about the entire area. As fate would have it, I believe it was meant to be that we met this man, called Leon.

He had been a Chief of Police in Danzig when the Red Army stormed the region, and he was immediately fired when they took over the city, along with the entire police force. He ended up teaching history, and was now retired, doing a little taxi driving to keep himself occupied. When I told him why I was there, and what I wanted to see, he told us that his son, Rafa, was also a history teacher, and he arranged to bring his son to the hotel to meet us that evening, as school was on break. The hotel was a charming converted Mill, in a stunning part of the countryside near Elblag. That evening, sure enough, Leon and Rafa turned up and we sat outside on a stone terrace overlooking the Mill-wheel turning in a running stream. They couldn't have been nicer or more helpful. I could say that I sensed they were almost excited that I was writing a book about the area. I explained exactly what I wanted to do, the areas I wanted to explore, and Rafa offered to take us anywhere I wanted to go the next day. He seemed to be as excited as we were that Ruth's memories were going to be retraced. True to his word, he picked us up after breakfast at the hotel the next morning and said he was ours for the day. What a wonderful day we had!

Fascinating is a mild word for all the things he told us about his own family's life during that day, well worth another book, to be sure, but when it came to my list of places Ruth had told me about, he took us to every single one. The schoolhouse; the water lilies on the river; the street on which Ruth had lived; the hill where she went with Brigette to look at the larks flying above them, and where they went tobogganing as children; the village Church; the railway line going to the ocean where her grandmother had taken her and Steven; the blue flowers Ruth remembered which grew all around the village; her uncle's farm where prisoners of war worked in the fields and the most horrific of all, the prison camp in Stutthof, where so many people had died. I took photographs of everything to give to Ruth, knowing she never would return. She was more emotional than I had ever seen her when I gave her those photos, and she told me she put them under her pillow and slept with them there every night.

During our many times together, mostly I didn't ask questions, I just listened and took countless notes. And then, after about six months we went away together, to the holiday home her daughter, Barbara, and son-in-law, Tavio, own in Georgia. During this time she really opened up to me. Now it was my turn to ask the questions and Ruth didn't hold back. There was always a sad side to Ruth. It was subtle, but in almost every word, every sentence, one could sense the sadness behind it. I needed to get to the truth, so one evening, sitting on the veranda of the cottage in Georgia, I asked her to tell me if what I had perceived in her, the sadness, was correct. She told me yes, that she had never stopped loving Commander Andersson. His influence on her was so profound, and of course intensified by the circumstances surrounding their relationship. But her loyalty and consideration for Karl, who had risked even his parents love, to go to America and begin a new life for her and Barbara, made her understand what true loyalty was.

Sadly, Ruth passed away on September 4th, 2017. Leaving behind beloved Barbara, her husband Tavio, and her adored grandson, Bryan.

Her story has now been told.

Dear Ruth: You can now rest in peace. Everyone understands, and loves you; and with a great deal of faith, I hope you are with Drews Andersson

THE END